MW01105872

"Linda J. Johnso
society that is lar
we are in the midst of two overseas wars. *Living in the Shadow of the Iraq Conflict: Our Story—From a Military Contractor's Wife* is a compelling and often poignant reality check that takes the reader on a roller coaster ride of human emotions. War strips away the comfortable veneer so carefully constructed by most people—a veneer that shields most Americans from the unpleasant and heartbreaking realities and emotional ups and downs lived daily by military and wartime contractor families. Author Johnson brings these realities and emotions out into the open—hope, fear, joy, frustration, anticipation, loneliness, and the strength of an abiding faith. By doing so, she presents an invitation to her fellow Americans to understand and embrace these very special families.

As the father of an army chaplain who has completed two tours of duty in Iraq and as a Vietnam veteran myself, I am well-acquainted with faraway, unpopular wars. So I know that Linda J. Johnson speaks with a loving confidence for thousands of families who are impacted every single day of their lives by the wars in Iraq and Afghanistan and the ongoing war against terrorism. I recommend her book for all who love our country and hold dear the faith that keeps America and American families strong."

L. Wayne Roberson
Lieutenant Colonel, USAF (Ret)
Cleveland, TN

"I believe that I was most touched by the hardships that Linda has gone through for the past three years. This book opened my eyes to an entire group of people who are sometimes forgotten but important to the grand scheme of America's 'war on terror.' *Living in the Shadow of the Iraq Conflict: Our Story—From a Military Contractor's Wife* kept my interest, and I would recommend this story of faith and commitment to all age groups."

Jeffrey Hayes, Senior Pastor
Faith Temple Church
Sioux Falls, SD

LIVING IN THE SHADOW OF THE
IRAQ CONFLICT

LIVING IN THE SHADOW OF THE
IRAQ CONFLICT

*Our Story—From a Military
Contractor's Wife*

LINDA J.JOHNSON

TATE PUBLISHING & Enterprises

Published by Tate Publishing & Enterprises, LLC
127 E. Trade Center Terrace | Mustang, Oklahoma 73064 USA
1.888.361.9473 | www.tatepublishing.com

Tate Publishing is committed to excellence in the publishing industry. The company reflects the philosophy established by the founders, based on Psalm 68:11,
"The Lord gave the word and great was the company of those who published it."

Book design copyright © 2009 by Tate Publishing, LLC. All rights reserved.
Cover design by Kandi Evans
Interior design by Nathan Harmony

Published in the United States of America

ISBN: 978-1-60799-304-9
1. Political Science: Political Freedom & Security: General
2. Biography & Autobiography: Military
09.01.28

DEDICATION

This book is being dedicated to all of those brave men and women who have sacrificed home and country to work inside Iraq or Afghanistan during a time of conflict. You have worked alongside our military, and I thank you for your valiant efforts. To the families left behind, I applaud your bravery and selfless dedication as you supported your loved ones in their decision to go.

Another reason I am writing this is for him. He will have a more cohesive and complete picture of what this journey has been like for me.

ACKNOWLEDGEMENTS

To: Charlotte, Linda D and Laurie, thank you for always standing behind Rich and I throughout this journey. You girls have been a source of comfort to both of us countless times. For this reason I ask that God will continue to bless your lives.

FOREWORD

In *Living in the Shadow of the Iraq Conflict*, Linda Johnson has shared her heart experiences and struggles for her and her husband while he is serving our country as a civilian/military contractor in Iraq. This book will help to set the record straight from many misunderstandings of just what the civilian/military contractors and their families go through.

She shares daily living, both for her as a wife keeping together a home and family and the life of her husband who is dedicated to helping our servicemen and women in their challenges while deployed to Iraq.

It is written to help those who have friends or family serving in Iraq, both military and civilian, and to help others who want to have a better understanding of what these families have to face.

What comes through loud and clear is her love for the

Lord and how he meets their daily needs while separated for long periods of time.

Manny Steele
State Representative, District 12
Sioux Falls, South Dakota

PREFACE

I remember that telephone call from Hawaii in February of 2004. Rich and I had just taken a week's vacation there the month before. We had reconnected with friends who were Filipino pastors that had recently immigrated to Hawaii from the Philippines. They had referred us to the bishop of our denomination for possible appointment. He called and offered us a position as co-pastors for a small Filipino fellowship on the island of Kauai. He asked us to prayerfully consider this appointment but couldn't offer us a salary or church building. This would be a ministry opportunity for us and a chance to heal from the negative experience of having had to flee the work in 1998. Rich turned it down at the time telling him, "Thank you; however, the timing isn't right."

Maybe the idea for my husband, Richard, to leave for Iraq was actually formulated back in 1998. We had gone to the Philippines that year to build and direct a training and mobilization center and seminary in the remote province of Aurora. This was not an unknown place to us. In fact, we had been there in the past as Christian missionaries, working among the people and establishing solid relationships in 1989 and again from 1992–94. We had also taken six American teams on short-term outreach to the Philippines during the years 1990–96 conducting follow up workshops and distributing relief goods through the local churches there.

The Filipino people, to us, were like family, and neither of us could foresee that in just eleven short months we would have to leave the project and flee for "fear of our personal safety." The plan to spend our twilight years among our adopted people ended abruptly and in chaos. We had received serious death threats from two different groups in the area—the communist rebels and Islamic radicals who had moved into town.

As we drew near to completing the upper floor of the seminary building, we noticed a subtle change of attitude from the local people. One of our adult students sent us a document and wanted to inform us that the Muslim families who had moved into the area were getting ready to build a training center, mosque, and school. This student wanted us to be aware that this group had petitioned the governor of the province for permission to begin construction immediately. They had also been pressuring the local Christian pastors and churches into "accepting" them.

Many of our pastors and churches had to be very careful not to offend these newcomers into the area, because they demanded the right to participate in and have an equal

  Linda J. Johnson

voice in all the business and religious gatherings in the province. Rich and I thought the tactic was very much like bullying, and we went about our work among the people despite these new concerns.

We held a meeting with the governor and his wife in private and gave him the names of the families that had moved into town from Mindanao. We warned him to take a very close look at the activities of this group and made him aware that some young women from the province had already been affected by marrying some of the new men moving in. These were Christian families, and their daughters were being married to men as second or third wives. This information had been given to us privately, and we passed it on to him.

The governor's wife explained to us that sometimes when people are desperate financially, they will give way to groups like this and that she wasn't sure what they could do to stop this threat. We sent the documents and names down to the U.S. Embassy in Manila through a runner and left the matter in their hands. We also asked them to advise us what to do, if anything.

Meanwhile, I was teaching religion courses pro bono in the school system and had heard from some of our teachers that the newcomers were very upset with my coursework concerning the exposure of Islamic beliefs. At the same time, the local NPA (new people's army) or communist groups began to pressure us at the center about our water use. They tapped illegally on to our water pipe system and then proceeded to do their laundry and resented it if we used the water and caused the flow to be interrupted.

We later learned that even though we made a rice drop

and distribution to these people as a gesture of goodwill and friendship, they were already receiving goods and finances from the Muslims and our mission was quite different from theirs. Both groups seemed to focus on stopping any and all activity in the province that did not promote either of their agendas (anti-government or pro-Islam).

A parent of one of our adult students came up to the province during this time from Zamboanga City and warned Rich and me that he had heard some talk at the market about us remaining there in peace and whether or not our work at the Christian center was necessary to the future of the region. This was a cause of alarm for us because earlier in the year an American Peace Corps worker had been killed in a provincial area of the Philippines. The newspapers were reporting that the Philippine government was advising any Americans out in provinces to be wary of any signs of mistrust in them working among the people. They were reporting that the safety of any Americans that might have a threat even implied against them could be compromised.

We received a visit one day in early November 1998 from one of my husband's close friends who was in the Philippine military stationed there. He came with the barangay captain (neighborhood watch authority) to inform us that we would be advised to hire an armed guard for the center. When we asked him why this would be necessary after all these years of building and establishing relationships there, he just told Rich, "Things and times change. I wouldn't want anything to happen to either of you or the staff here." We couldn't believe that our only choice to remain there would be to hire armed guards for a Christian seminary and training center at this point in the project.

We sent another runner to Manila with this information, and we received word back that we were to make ready to leave the province. We were instructed to pack six to eight boxes of our belongings and to tell no one that we would be evacuated within the next week. Our contact in Manila would send one of her men from the office of whom was known to us, along with armed drivers, and we were to leave the province immediately.

We were evacuated very early in the morning on a cold, rainy, and windy day at the end of November. The roads down the mountain had been washed out from frequent typhoons that season, and we were fortunate that we got out when we did.

We had one of our Filipino staff with us, and she stayed with us in Manila at a safe house while we were processed out of the Philippines. This process took over three weeks until we were flown to Hawaii. In Hawaii, Rich and I rested and awaited the arrival of our children and my mother to have a belated Christmas there.

We left Hawaii mid-January 1999 bound back to Kansas City and moved back into our old parsonage. We were devastated by the loss of the work in the Philippines.

I don't believe that we ever fully recovered emotionally, mentally, or financially from that experience. It was a life-changing experience for us and a pivotal point in our journey.

CHAPTER 1

Although we returned to Kansas City in January 1999 from the Philippines and Rich was welcomed back at his work as a mechanic/trainer for Midas muffler, we couldn't seem to recover financially. With me being on full disability and also suffering from PTSD (post traumatic stress disorder) due to the events surrounding our leaving the Philippines, it grew even harder to meet all of our needs. It appeared to us that we would be relegated to playing catch up, financially, for the rest of our lives.

We discussed the possibilities of which direction our lives should take. We decided to "stay the course" in Kansas City. Rich felt this was necessary to stabilize my health. I had been in a bad place again with pain cycles and unknown complications—due to an undiagnosed thyroid disorder—on top of my syndrome X disability. This is a heart/kidney-related chronic illness that is hereditary. So we regretfully called our friends on Oahu and the bishop over Hawaii and explained our decision and asked them to pray for us.

The summer of 2004 found us living in a small apartment nearby to Rich's workplace. He would come home for lunch many days. He would also test drive the vehicles right by our place. He would honk and wave as he drove by, while I hung clothes outside on the line on our patio. He was actually checking up on me, since I was now more alone than at any other time in our lives. It became his responsibility that spring and summer to provide for our needs and watch over me and my health problems.

We took care of our grandchildren, Jada and Chase, occasionally during that time and had a few other activities going on around Kansas City. However, something was missing again from our lives. We didn't feel fulfilled.

Linda J. Johnson

CHAPTER 2

In August of 2004, our Filipino pastoral friends from Oahu's North Shore came to Kansas City for a visit. They were on the mainland for a convention in Texas. They encouraged us to rethink our decision to take the missions assignment on Kauai. This time they explained that the outgoing pastor was a relative of theirs who was leaving Kauai. He had organized a new fellowship on the Big Island, and they needed a replacement couple for their group. They thought we would be able to work with the people and take over what he had started due to our background. They asked us to consider devoting a couple of years to evaluating and leading the group there. We thought that it would be a good place for my body to heal, as well as fill in the void missing from our lives.

Probably the hardest part of that decision to move, besides the unknown and selling off some of our furniture, was packing up boxes again. We also didn't realize what a negative impact this move would have on our granddaughter, Jada, three-and-a-half years old at that time. I will always believe that our leaving at that point in her life crushed her little spirit.

The movers had come on a Thursday. We also had a missionary friend visiting from South Dakota. Marian Gustafson was helping us pack. She had loaded some boxes into her car to take back to South Dakota to store for us. As we watched the movers load everything on the crate, we somehow lost track of Jada. I found her face down on the carpet of our bedroom, and she was crying her eyes out. She said, "Grandma, those men took all of you and Grandpa's stuff. They even took your bed and my things out of my room." Jada had stayed a lot with us during her young life. It was heartbreaking for her, and she just didn't understand why this was happening. She was already missing all of the good times in our house, and now this!

I tried my best to calm her down, but she only wanted her grandpa. He took her out to the grocery store, and she got to pick out her favorite purple gum and a box of candies. She had the utmost love for her grandpa. Anytime she got upset, Grandpa could always be counted on to get her smiling and laughing again. Grandpa told her that maybe she could come to Hawaii soon with her mommy and daddy and Chase and live there with us. We both actually believed that this was a real possibility.

As we dropped her off later on that day, at her other grandma's house, we had no idea we wouldn't see her again until January of 2006 on the island of Kauai. Her little life seemed to be in as much of turmoil as ours was that day.

My sister Marcia, who lived in Kansas City, hosted us at

Linda J. Johnson

her house until our plane departed four days later. Rich and I look back and realize how helpful Marcia became to us during that time. She knew we were paying off medical bills and other debts that we hadn't caught up on from restarting our lives in 1999. She also knew that our denomination's assignment for us to Kauai would only include a part of our expenses to ship our household goods there.

Also, we told her there was no salary offered and that the fellowship only had a small apartment for us to live in, because that was all they could afford. It was truly another missionary assignment for us. But we made the decision in the hopes that my health problems would stabilize, and we would be back in full-time ministry to answer our calling.

Marcia chose to "pay it forward." She gave us a generous financial gift to help us offset the upcoming expenses of the move. Little did she know her gift would keep us afloat financially while Rich searched for full-time employment on Kauai, which was another surprise that we hadn't planned on! We really didn't know that we would arrive on Kauai and discover that we had no permanent home and no job to be had for Rich.

With her generosity we were also able to pay off our portion of the cost of the shipping of our household goods. We were also able to pay off a new computer that we had purchased the previous year. The computer turned out to be the only one we had to use for the entire fellowship, used almost exclusively to support the families of the fellowship while we were there. Most of our fellowship members had neither the expertise nor the finances to purchase their own, let alone learn how to run it at the time. So what Marcia did for us was nothing short of a miracle!

CHAPTER 3

The culture shock we experienced when arriving on Kauai would continue throughout our stay there. Who could have known that the local people of this island had an attitude problem towards outsiders (especially *haoles*, or white outsiders)? It was déjà vu for us all over again, like the experiences we had first encountered in the southern Philippines back in 1993. What I thought was "reverse prejudice" was actually an intense racist attitude that permeates throughout the state of Hawaii. This attitude is going on up to now between the races, with a lot of hostility being directed towards white people.

The adjustment was difficult for us both. Rich had to deal with prejudice on a day-to-day basis whenever it reared its ugly head at the job site. A perfect example of racial inequity came up when he first got on Kauai and went to the Chrysler dealership to get his start date for work. The promised job at that dealership was given to a local instead of to my husband. He was devastated. After applying for employment for six weeks, he finally went to work as a tech specialist at Ford Motor Company.

Our being embedded within the Filipino community on Kauai helped us out in this regard. Mostly the Filipino people took us under their wings and accepted us as one of their own, despite the misgivings they may have had about crossing the cultural gap.

Imagine Rich's and my shock when we realized that we would be housed in a four-generation home of Filipinos. The owner of the house was a mixed race of Japanese and Hawaiian descent. The family wasn't part of the fellowship that we were now leading. The house was just located in the same neighborhood as some of our members with convenient access to everyone. Our six-hundred-square-feet apartment was even opened up to the family downstairs. We would have no total privacy for the next two years. We were connected to their main house by an open staircase only. We did have a separate entrance outside. So we learned, once again, to coexist with strangers under one roof.

The AhPuck family adjusted to us, and we adjusted to them. Their family would become a huge blessing to us, as they opened up their hearts and home for the entire time we lived on Kauai. Rich and I have only fond memories of our relationship with them. I know he felt they would take care of me when he left, and that is why he was able to make the ultimate decision to go to Iraq in 2005, while we still lived there.

Not long after Rich began employment at the Ford dealership in December of 2004, he became panicked over his wages. He recognized that he would have a difficult time earning the equivalent of his pay in Kansas City. There were only so many people on the small island, and Rich saw most of the business coming in as warranty work. His pay was not going to cover our bills, let alone our living expenses.

Everyone in Hawaii, except for us, was aware of the higher cost of living. From groceries to gas and everyday necessity items, we were all expected to pay more (much more), because after all, Kauai was a remote place. Much of our produce and staples were shipped to the island from Hawaii or from the mainland to Honolulu and re-shipped to Kauai. (Kauai more or less sits off by itself northwest of Oahu and Honolulu.)

Although Kauai is a paradise and popular destination for vacationers worldwide, it is an expensive place for locals to live, work, and raise their families. We began to understand why most of the families in our fellowship worked multiple jobs. They lived with more than one generation in their homes. This was an economic lifestyle choice for most of the people throughout Hawaii, in order to just get by and meet obligations.

The flipside was of course that their choice afforded them a beautiful ocean and island-living, and they were envied by people worldwide for where they lived. What a paradox! Most of our families worked in the tourism industry and made their living off of the people who vacationed there. Some of our tourists had saved for months to come to Kauai, and many believed that they would find the perfect vacation spot; weddings, wedding anniversaries, and family reunions took place there regularly.

We got to see the hardship of the locals and their concerns for their future up close and personal. They were also very concerned for the future of their children and whether their kids would ever be able to afford to live on Kauai. The islands were losing their young people to the mainland in big numbers due to economics. Even housing began to show signs of "shaking," as Hawaiian homes for sale stayed on the market much longer than in previous years.

Rich and I knew in the first few months we would never afford a larger place to rent, and certainly it would be impractical to consider ever buying a house on Kauai! They were simply too expensive. Further, it appeared the fellowship itself would not be able to evolve into an actual church on Kauai. We couldn't get over the fact that the position appeared to be misrepresented when presented to us. If we were to buy property for a church, it would cause a burden or hardship for our people. It was a stark reality check.

We also learned that our denomination had no plans to expand on Kauai (at least not if they had to invest financially). It would be up to us to guide our people into the reality that their own future as an independent church was not going to be possible. We now had to get past the realization that we had been misled. We had a choice—pack up and leave or stay with our people and keep our commitment to this group. We stayed.

It was a great heartache for us to know that our people had their hearts set on their own building. They even wanted an all-in-one building that could house their pastor and hold services. But we knew that there were no funds available for them or even allocated for their future. The small savings that they had accumulated since their humble beginnings wouldn't be enough to reach their goals. This didn't keep us from confronting our bishop with ideas and suggestions as to how to accomplish that goal. However, it wasn't to be.

Throughout Hawaii, it was the same story for workers in our denomination. Pastors were working and living in rental units and even sharing church buildings with one another, holding services at different hours. Rich began to look at his options for all of us, right after the holiday season of 2004. We were sharing a building with the Baptists, and he was frustrated both with his work and with our denomination. He felt that they had let us down and didn't have a real concern for us, nor would they commit to future plans for our people. We could determine through conversations at the state level that there were no plans for a building project for us on Kauai. In short, we were left on our own to sort it all out.

We had committed at least two years to this fellowship, and now we were running out of our own personal finances. What could we do to keep our promises and pay for our own financial obligations? It was a dilemma we hadn't planned on when we accepted the assignment. We didn't want to burden the families of the fellowship with our personal budget short-falls, especially when they were responsible in their financial obligations to the church and their own commitments.

We found that they were very willing and able to furnish our apartment, utilities, and all the expenses of running the business of the church. We were also going to keep their savings intact, which they wanted to use later on to build a building.

Their giving increased, and we remained responsible to the denomination for the ongoing projects that had been adopted by the group ahead of our joining them. We were even able to increase denominational support throughout our assignment!

We always believed that in the giving of our resources and time generously, somehow our own personal needs would be met.

  Linda J. Johnson

CHAPTER 4

One of the first major projects we tackled on the island was organizing an island-wide response reaching out to Aurora Province in the Philippines. We had received news that a devastating typhoon had destroyed much of the infrastructure and food crops there. The people were in need of basic items like clothing and food.

For two weeks we collected goods in kind from all over the island. The local newspaper published the plea, and we were able to send over fifty boxes to the people affected. The local Filipino shipper gave us discounted rates and only charged his fees for the boxes, and the Filipino Ministers' Association underwrote a great majority of the shipping charges. It was a morale booster for our people to be involved in helping out those Filipinos who were in great need. Our denomination featured this project as a news story on our

Faith News Network. We were beginning the ministry there on an upbeat mode.

The next big event for us personally was when our oldest son, Frank, and his family came to visit us in January of 2005. We had a wonderful week with the grandchildren, and the weather cooperated. We enjoyed the quality family time.

Frank and his family gifted our fellowship with a beautiful communion set, and the Filipino community of churches welcomed and embraced his family wholeheartedly. This is always the *aloha* of Hawaii.

Frank and his family never realized that his dad had already come to the realization that he wouldn't be able to earn enough money to support us while working on Kauai. He was only earning two-thirds of his salary requirements due to less demand for vehicle work at the Ford dealership. He told me there were only so many vehicles, and most of the work coming in was warranty work, which didn't pay commission for him. Furthermore, Rich said that at that rate he would either have to take a second job to meet our personal budget or we would have to consider moving back to the mainland.

We were also aware of the looming housing problems that were surfacing already on Kauai, and housing for us personally was too expensive to purchase and out of our reach. Even the possibility of purchasing land to build a multi-purpose building did not seem possible as we exhausted every avenue within our denomination factored in with the savings our fellowship had. We were out of options. We knew almost immediately that our recommendation for them would be that they merge with a sister church on the island

and strengthen each other in the days ahead and combine congregations and resources for the good of all.

We knew that it was a sensitive topic to our fellowship, and we wanted to spend the needed time it would take to guide them into the mindset whereby they would come to this same decision.

In April of 2005, Rich saw an ad in *USA Today*. A major military contractor was advertising for wheel mechanics to go to Iraq as military/army contractors.

As we came to learn more about this, during 2004 and 2005, numerous Defense Department contracting companies were sending in civilians and recruiting actively to meet contract quotas. In the case of Lear Siegler Inc., they needed technicians who would fill in a gap for the army. The MOS (military occupation specialty) was actually wheeled mechanic. From what we understand, this MOS has continued to be a critical job shortage for the army up to today.

We believe that 70% of the men deployed during these years to Iraq or Afghanistan in this capacity have been vets who had either been deployed during Desert Storm (1991) or never been deployed during a time of war, so it was a new experience for many of them.

At the time, however, we didn't know yet or understand the differences between contractors and the variety of roles or positions they would fill inside the combat zones. All of that would become clearer later.

Rich sent in a résumé and thought there wouldn't be any harm in checking on these positions. He had never been able to go to Vietnam because the draft had stopped, and he thought it would be better to stay at home on the farm to help even though all of his brothers had served in one capacity or another during that era.

Also during the early years of our marriage, army recruiters discouraged him from enlisting because they felt he might receive a medical waiver due to the preventative medications that he had been taking since a childhood fall. Although Rich had not had any problems since that injury, he gave up on the possibility of going career military.

In Houston, when he explained this to the medical doctors during his processing for Iraq, they didn't see it as an issue at all! So Rich would finally get to "do his part" in this way. He has felt that he is a part of something much bigger than himself in the support of OIF (Operation Iraqi Freedom). Although he doesn't wear the uniform, he is right in the midst of all the action or at the front there in Baghdad. He was committed to the U.S. cause in Iraq from the first day he stepped foot in there and remains that committed today.

Some of our families on Kauai were affected personally now as well by the Iraq conflict. The National Guard of Kauai had been activated for deployment during the autumn of 2004. We were following closely what was happening to them through the experiences of caring for and backing up our church clerk. She and her three kids were left behind while her husband was deployed. He would be stationed at Liberty/Victory Base in Baghdad.

Rich gave a pledge to her husband that he and I would watch over and support his wife and three kids left behind while he deployed for one year to Iraq. We knew and could feel her deep sense of loss in giving up her husband and putting their lives on hold for the days ahead. On the flip side,

  Linda J. Johnson

we all displayed a great sense of pride in the service of the Kauai National Guard for what their role would be in Iraq.

During that timeframe, we were all also nervous for his safety. We pulled together, however, and focused on supporting him and his family to help make their separation easier. This was a young family, and Rich and I could sense and feel their fear and the emotional turmoil they were going through. Little did we know we would soon face the same thing.

Rich was also concerned at that time for me because I was scheduled for a thyroid surgery coming up soon in Honolulu. We would have medical bills again, and he wasn't sure we could cope with the pressures and demands upon us at the time in addition to managing financial difficulties. We were quite sure all of this would affect my health adversely.

In May of 2005, I was admitted to Straub Clinic at Honolulu for further diagnostic testing and a heart-health checkup. I ended up having an angiogram once again for the heart and a renal scan for the kidneys. We then realized that a lot of the health care I would need in the future couldn't be done on Kauai. We knew that for our long-term future, Kauai would not be the place we could settle permanently.

Unfortunately, May of 2005 also gave us another challenge. We had been out to our favorite beach on a Saturday, enjoying a shoreline swim. Out of nowhere a rogue wave, or unusual wave, came off the ocean, swept both of us up into the air, and slammed me back onto the shoreline. I was injured with a compressed disc in my lower back that day and was thankful that it hadn't come to anything worse.

This injury is not able to be treated other than by using a back machine nightly, along with rehab exercises learned in therapy, to keep my lower back from excruciating pain and me from immobility. We were both thankful that nothing worse happened. It took me more than three weeks to get back into my walking routine and regain my strength.

From that day forward, I never ventured into the ocean from a beach that wasn't walled in by rock. I had gained a newfound respect for the unpredictability of the ocean and the fact that my strength couldn't compete against it! All of the horror stories that we would hear from that point on regarding people and their encounters with that ocean we believed wholeheartedly and were able to empathize. There were quite a few incidents of drowning and water accidents, involving tourists, during the two years we were on Kauai.

In addition, during May of 2005, Rich received a phone call from a company recruiter for Lear Siegler. This man was responsible to fill the positions inside Iraq, and he had determined that Rich's qualifications fit the job description and matched the need for a wheeled mechanic position. One of the other reasons they were considering hiring Rich, other than his years of experience as a mechanic, was because he had lived in harsh conditions in third world countries as a missionary.

He told Rich to expect a package from FedEx. This mailing would contain a contract and application form for Rich to complete. He was supposed to fill it all out and send it back in immediately. If they were interested in him, they would get back to him with a conference call.

When the next recruiter called with Rich's completed package, he asked him the status of his passport. It was due to expire. He was on his third passport already. They told us to expedite it for his full processing. He was supposed to

  Linda J. Johnson

keep the receipt, as it would eventually be reimbursed. We did that on Kauai and asked for a delay from the company to begin employment at the beginning of August of 2005. This would give us time to prepare our people and to take a stateside trip to see family. We wanted to put our affairs in order. Also, this would give Rich ample time to give a notice to his employer.

The company agreed that Rich could be accepted into the first week of August classes at Houston. They wanted him to be ready for a call by the end of July for final instructions. They would then give him his date to report, along with information on how to procure his prepaid airline ticket. We would be using an agency in Denver, Colorado, that was contracted by the company.

CHAPTER 5

While Rich and I were sure that we had made the right decision, I began to prepare myself for what was to come. We had decided that I would be able to lead the fellowship with the help of our district overseer and our associate pastor for another year. We did believe that Rich would only sign on for one year at that time.

On a Sunday afternoon in May, after our morning services, we received a phone call from the state bishop's office. The bishop's wife asked us to proceed to the hospital because she had gotten a call from Mississippi. There had been a drowning on Kauai involving a family from our denomination. We rushed to the hospital only to be told that the victim was a male, aged fifty years old, and they had sent the new widow and her ten-year-old daughter back to their hotel! I was shocked. No one was yet with them.

Rich and I had gotten the phone call in the first place because the decedent was a youth pastor from one of our denominational churches in Jackson, Mississippi. They were vacationing on Kauai, and their senior pastor back in Mississippi was frantic to be able to get spiritual care to this couple and their young daughter at this time of tragedy. We had no idea how involved we would become personally in this family's life.

I reached her cell phone and told her we were on the way to her. When we arrived, it was very, very sad. Apparently her husband had expired while snorkeling in shallow water. He had probably had a heart attack and then drowned as a result. This happened in full view of a crowded beach, and the wife was overcome with grief. Rich and I spent all afternoon with her and her daughter, and we called our district overseer to come stay with them while we conducted our evening services at the Baptist church.

Before leaving we promised her we would return, and then I gave instructions to the other couple. I told them to continue to talk her down and get her to the point of packing their things. I knew she was so far from home and would want to go back home as soon as the initial shock wore off. Our district overseer and his wife ministered to them and got them to get some practical chores done. They also contacted one of our ministers in Honolulu who worked in a mortuary. He phoned the funeral home that was to receive the body and gave instructions to them.

When we returned to her hotel, she was ready to just sit, talk, and show us pictures on their digital camera, already loaded onto her laptop. The pictures were taken not a half

  Linda J. Johnson

hour before he died. At that point I thought maybe modern technology wasn't so great. The viewing of these pictures caused her so much pain and grief.

We wrote out a list of things for her to do the next day, Monday. I believed that this would occupy her and her daughter and keep them moving so they wouldn't collapse into so much grief and pain that they would shut down. Then I just listened as she reminisced about what could have been. It was so very heartbreaking.

When we got back to the pastoral house, I worked the phones with United Airlines for the better part of three hours. Finally I reached an agreement with them to ship the body on the original ticket the husband had flown out on. They also told me they would make special provisions for the mother and daughter during their travel back to Mississippi. I relayed this to her home church pastor in Mississippi. He felt so helpless throughout this early stage of the tragedy. I assured him that everyone was working to get her home, along with the body, as soon as possible.

The next day I drove down to her hotel to pick up her daughter while our district pastor took her to the funeral home to make final arrangements for the body. Our downstairs neighbor, Shirley, picked up Rich from work in Lihue and then drove him down to pick up the Jeep so I could stay with the mother and daughter. I later dropped off her rental car, which was nearby to Rich's work place. I was able to tell him how it went before going home to bed.

United Airlines gave us a special waiting lounge at Kauai airport, and she, her daughter, and I were able to take as much time as she needed before boarding. The entire plane waited for her while she processed that she was going to have to leave her husband behind and go without him. I have to admit that the United Airlines crew and staff there went overboard to accommodate us, and they were so gentle with her and her daughter.

Finally she was ready to go, and the airline's crew allowed me to board with her. The pilot on this flight going to Chicago had placed his wife, who had been vacationing on Kauai, in the row of three seats that the mother and daughter would occupy. I was so very thankful that they would have a companion who would shelter them from others during the flight and understand the grieving that would occur. It was very hard to leave them on that plane. With tear-stained faces, we hugged and promised to see each other again soon. I made a promise to her that her husband would follow shortly (the body).

In fact, the husband's body did leave Kauai in just two short days, and this new widow was able to bury him in Mississippi by Thursday. This in itself was a miracle. This tragedy and the ensuing events took a huge emotional and physical toll upon me. I stayed in bed for two days after she left. We would, in fact, reunite later that year in Mississippi. We formed a very strong bond.

I had my thyroid surgery on Kauai in June of 2005, and we planned a trip stateside for July. While we traveled to the mainland to transport some boxes for storage, I was still recovering from the surgery. The surgeons had found an undetected lump, or growth, on the thyroid, and this had caused a lot of my health problems during the previous two years in Kansas City. Thankfully, when the labs returned, we found out that it had been non-cancerous!

We went to say good-bye to our son Chris and our grandchildren, Jada and Chase, in Kansas City. We also made a one-week road trip to South Dakota to see our families and then flew back to the islands from Sioux Falls. It was a fast and furious trip.

Once again, my sister hosted us in Kansas City. We were also able to spend a day with Chris and his kids. They were so happy to see Grandpa. The temperatures outside were in triple digits, and it appeared this would be a sign of what was to come for Rich in the days ahead. We enjoyed those few nights with family and visited old friends.

Once we left Kansas City, we drove north up I-29 toward South Dakota. Rich wanted to say good-bye to his family living in South Dakota before he left for Iraq. He has three sisters, one brother, and extended family living near Sioux Falls.

I remember clearly the day we were visiting my mom, July 25, 2005, at Mitchell, South Dakota. We had gone to the Corn Palace to buy South Dakota gifts for our youth group back on Kauai. Rich finally got the important phone call. He would be expected at Houston, Texas, on August 5, 2005. We asked if his airline ticket could originate on Kauai, with an overnight stop in Honolulu. The human resources representative told Rich that it was up to him. As long as he arrived in Houston sometime on August 5, he could leave Kauai at any time and stop over at Honolulu. That was the only routing available anyway. There weren't any direct flights to Houston from Kauai.

We began to call everyone to let them know of Rich's

impending deployment. The only thing we knew about his time in Houston was that he would be fast-tracked to Iraq. He would also receive full physical and medical exams and be trained in safety. He would be issued gear for chemical warfare and a fully-sealed suit. What we understood about fast-track was that he would not spend much time in Houston but be shipped out as soon as possible to Iraq.

I copied all the contract papers that Richard had already signed and made notes on all the benefits choices he had made or would have to make. Later on, I would use these same papers we had filled out in May, while he was at Houston, to compare any differences with the new paperwork. I began a file for him of these very important papers.

  Linda J. Johnson

CHAPTER 6

On July 27, 2005, we flew out of Sioux Falls to go back to Kauai, I wondered just when Rich would ever be in South Dakota again. During the long flight, both of us talked about whether we were ready to cope with this kind of change. This would be the first time in twenty-eight years of marriage that we would be facing a long separation. Our plan was for Rich to contract for one year. We thought this would help us get our debts paid down and enable us to complete our commitment on Kauai.

Rich really felt there wasn't any way we could remain on Kauai without him taking this job. That airline ride back to Kauai was bittersweet as we discussed everything in detail and began to prepare ourselves for a completely different type of marriage relationship, one that would be sustained through many miles and many months apart.

We drew up a power of attorney the minute we got back on Kauai. Once again, our church clerk proved to be an invaluable help to us at that time because she was familiar with this already. She had had to do this, just like many military spouses left behind. We were able to execute this, and it is the second most valuable document I have used since the day he left. Only his orders would supersede this as more valuable for me to keep in a special file at home.

I would be asked for his power of attorney to pay our utilities, take money from our bank accounts, and pay credit card payments. Our license plate renewal couldn't even be completed in the State of Hawaii without that power of attorney!

One of the next things we did when we arrived back on Kauai was to call our associate pastor. We invited him over for a visit and discussed our plans with him. Rich asked him to be available to me as much as possible in the upcoming days. This would be the only way I could stay on Kauai for another year. Pastor Gomez was vital to the ministry, and Rich was relying on him to help me. Pastor Gomez understood our dilemma because he too, in the past, had left his family in the Philippines. He had worked in Saudi Arabia for a time for the sake of his family's finances.

Our bishop at Honolulu was supportive and prayed with Rich and me over our decision. He would later call Rich in Houston and encourage him, as well as e-mail him occasionally in Iraq to see how he was doing. He always asked about him during phone calls to me. The bishop was very pleased that I would stay on and commit myself to the work on Kauai with the fellowship rather than abandon them.

We had called the designated travel agency, and we

  Linda J. Johnson

arranged to spend two nights in Honolulu. We stayed with some colleagues there. The Bocobo family hosted us and took us to the airport for Rich's departure to Houston. These were some of the most difficult days in our lives.

Everything changed for us after August 5. I stayed in Honolulu until the next day and waited for Rich's first phone call from Houston. We were so thankful for such good friends, who are like family to us.

We had spent July 27 to August 3 packing Rich's bags. Our church clerk had given him an army duffel bag that had been her husband's. He took that to Houston, along with his carry-on bag. We packed according to the instructions and lists provided (jeans, T-shirts, jackets, and the all-important steel-toe boots). We also packed a six-month supply of his medicines and personal hygiene items, per the instructions.

He took our largest carry-on. He was really loaded down, but we were practiced in packing for strange places! We believed he was prepared to rough it. Once again, we are thankful this was ahead of the new TSA regulations and the 3–1-1 rules. When Chris processed with the company the following year, he had to ship a box ahead to his dad's base. This was the only way he could get enough personal supplies in.

Rich finally arrived in Houston, and he was picked up at the airport and taken to his hotel. After in-processing, he went to sleep. Rich had the unique distinction of being the man in his class who traveled the farthest distance to get to training! He was also a mystery to so many of the guys because he was so quiet. They later told him that they thought he was either a minister or a hired gun! (Well, they got the minister part right!)

Rich told me that all of his company's personnel working with him would be men, but some women were included at the Houston training classes. Most of the females would be going to work for the largest contracting company recruiting American employees to deploy to Iraq. A few spouses were in Houston as well to see their husbands off. Later, I thought that this is what I should've done.

What we saw from the beginning of this job with this company was that there was a huge disconnect from the hiring personnel and their recruiting personnel. The recruiter and the trainees on the ground at Houston had a completely different understanding of how it was going to play out. It became a new ballgame from that point on. It was very stressful for us, and probably for all of the families involved.

As a matter of fact, to this day, if Rich or I phone anyone in the States with questions on any subject, it gets back to Iraq. There is a rank and file within the company, and an employee is actually discouraged from getting any explanations or asking any questions in the U.S.A. about what is going on in Iraq for them. Everything must be done through the administration on-site, inside Iraq. It is confusing, discouraging, and very complicated at times. Rich and I have discussed so often that Iraq runs Iraq. Although he is an American employee of an American company, he is bound by Americans running the contract within Iraq. They have the same mindset as the military when it comes to stepping over the chain of command!

Day one in Houston brought changes to everything that we thought had already been taken care of. Rich was required to fill out brand-new benefits election sheets and new emer-

  Linda J. Johnson

gency contact sheets. He was so stressed out. We had already completed his forms together. Another rule change that came up in Houston was that they decided to tell the men that their pay wouldn't start until they were en route to Iraq. (This was called "wheels up.")

We were never told that. None of the recruiters had mentioned that fact. Like many families there, we too live on a budget. Rich had already left his job at Ford three weeks earlier, and now we weren't sure when his first paycheck would arrive. They told the guys they would be advancing them $200 for their travel to Iraq. This would then be deducted from their first paycheck. "Expect the unexpected" appeared to be the standard operating procedure and the rule of the day for these guys.

We had also told the initial recruiters in Fayetteville, Georgia, that Rich was interested in being assigned to Liberty/Victory Base. The National Guard unit from Kauai was stationed there, and Rich wanted to be where they were. The human resources office in Georgia had told Rich to just request that placement. Rich would find out later that it wasn't quite that simple. The company stateside operates completely differently from the company itself in Iraq. Rich would never see our Kauai unit in Iraq.

As I look back at that time now, I have to laugh at how naïve we were about this whole "contracting" process. We believed everything they told us. We even believed that Rich would earn $84,000 per year. No, it would never happen that way, and it wasn't even possible if they took their scheduled leaves. They conveniently forgot to mention our portion of the cost of his airline tickets for any leave and the difference in pay when, or if, they took their leaves.

In Houston, as Rich processed through his medical exam, he noticed some guys were eliminated right then and there. Apparently they weren't healthy enough, or the doctors decided against putting them through. Rich was issued his own gas mask and protection gear, to be used in the event of chemical warfare. He received multiple shots and inoculations. I kept asking him to send me copies of everything he signed, because all of the paperwork was null and voided. We were thankful to the hotel front desk because they faxed everything to me, and I started a new file!

At this point he didn't even know what his base pay would be. We had a contract in front of us, at home, that set his base hourly rate at $17.94. Later, when he arrived in Iraq, he found out his base pay would be $14.90 per hour, with "uplifts" for hazard pay and a Foreign Service bonus.

We also learned that Rich would have $1,000 deducted from his first five paychecks. If he made it for six months into contract, he would get the $5,000 reimbursed! What a shock! Imagine. Now, not only was there an initial-adjustment trial period in a war zone, but there would be incredible pressure to perform in Iraq. It all boiled down to "no choices." Once they left Houston, they were at the mercy of their supervisors, site managers, and those who were in charge. It seemed that at the whim of anyone above them, our guys could succeed or fail in Iraq.

We begin to realize that Rich had left a successful career as a top mechanic and walked into the unknown. He had been earning a fair wage, and he was being promoted at Ford.

  Linda J. Johnson

Unlike many of the men who were in Houston with him, he had been steadily employed all of his adult life.

CHAPTER 7

When Rich got closer to leaving Houston for Iraq, we got nervous. Our lives were changing right before our eyes. We would be sacrificing companionship, communication, and the "normal" married lifestyle. Nothing would be the same again. We would both change in the days, months, and years ahead.

All in all, Rich spent seven full days in Houston and was fast-tracked to Iraq. He informed me that after he shut his phone off on the airport runway, I probably wouldn't hear from him for a few days. I remember that last call, on August 12, 2005. I think we talked all the way through the pilots' greeting! Rich was on his way to Dubai via London.

Dubai, in United Arab Emirates, is the connecting city and pick-up and drop-off point for military contractors working in Iraq. It has actually become a very important city in the Middle East. Dubai is actually one of the friendlier and more open cities for Westerners, and Americans in particular. The hostility towards non-Arabs doesn't seem to be as apparent or evident there, as in the neighboring countries. The people of Dubai actually seem to court foreigners' business. They understand the importance of being a player in a global society.

Of course, along with the excitement of hosting Westerners connected to Iraq, there is a darker tale to tell. As Rich later told me, he observed the open drinking and partying and watched young girls being "sold" outright. More than once, Rich left the hotel they were housed at and went straight to the airport on the shuttle to avoid this scene.

It was very normal procedure in Dubai for the men to get a room and await their paperwork. They would then be put on the roster for transport back into the war zone. As he describes the process, I'm amazed at how smoothly it usually goes with so many men moving through there daily. There's no question that the conflict in Iraq and our men moving in and out through Dubai has contributed to their rising economy. This has also helped establish them as a destination place in the Middle East.

Now, back on Kauai, that second week of August 2005, while Rich was in Houston, I was adjusting to the reality that he was really gone. My partner, my lover, and my friend wouldn't be there daily. He wouldn't share meals with me anymore. He wouldn't be calling my phone anymore to just chat for a while. I don't think I washed our bedding for two weeks or more. I just wanted to keep his pillowcase on his pillow forever, because I could smell his aftershave there.

It took a long, long time for me to realize that when I rolled over in the bed, he wouldn't be there. I would wake up often during the night, and many a morning, with a dread of facing another day without him. We had been joined at the hip, so to speak. We had also lived in many remote places. Now we were going to face some tough days ahead, but not together.

I had been used to being a part of his daily decision-making, and he'd been a part of mine. We would both learn in the days to come to only bother each other with the big decisions in life. It was like withdrawal for me. My faith in my decision-making wavered a lot in those first few months. I'm really glad we didn't have more than a one-year plan at that time for this new venture. Neither of us would have been able to handle the thought of a longer separation back then.

Those first ten days that he was gone were the hardest for me of our entire married life. I was like a fish out of water even going to the grocery store. Questions and challenges came every day, something simple like, "How much food do I buy if it's only me at home?" How much and how often would I change the oil for the car? I remember spending an hour or two reading our Jeep's manual trying to find a lever that would open the hood.

I started a journal just for him and wrote personal notes to him. Oftentimes I was in tears knowing that I would forget a lot of daily experiences and never get to share them with him.

Surprisingly, he called from Dubai on August 13, 2005. We spent less than five minutes on that phone call. One of the guys in his class had some international minutes left on a phone card and had given it to Rich. He wanted me to know that he was okay. He told me that they would be picked up there, bound for Iraq.

I waited four days for his next call. It seemed like an

eternity! On August 17, 2005, he called from Anaconda Base inside Iraq. He didn't sound good on that call. They were all being separated and sent different directions. Anaconda and Liberty/Victory Bases were full and taking no more mechanics. Once again, the men realized "Iraq runs Iraq!" Rich told me it was completely chaotic. They were all having a rough time. He was so tense and stressed out. He told me that they felt like cattle.

He and three of the men were assigned to D-2, in Baghdad's Green Zone. They would transport them by "rhino" at night to get them to their destination. He explained that a "rhino" was a steel-plated vehicle. It was like a small bus, but steel-plated. They would have a military, armed escort to get into the job site. We later learned that the four miles of road between Baghdad's airport and the IZ zone (international zone) was one of the most dangerous stretches of road in Iraq. Rich would travel that road many, many times in the months and years ahead.

The best way to describe site D-2 was described to me by Rich as follows: "D-2, known as Camp Prosperity, is located in Baghdad's Green Zone and is an organization level maintenance team. Most of the customers (army) are not located on the FOB (field operating base) and must traverse some distances to reach the facility. Some are on direct missions and plan for a maintenance stop as they pass through. As such, these units do not have the luxury of long waits for maintenance and servicing for their respective vehicles, so the team at D-2 are the perfect group for the task! D-2 is a 'one-stop shop' if you will."

CHAPTER 8

Upon arrival in the Green Zone, they were first housed at FOB Union III and Grey Wolf. At that time, in August of 2005, inside Iraq, conditions for housing were constantly changing and evolving. They all scrambled for rooms in a large three-story building. Rich was assigned to work with the Georgians.

I remember when he first told me this, I couldn't understand if he meant an army unit from Georgia. Later, I realized this was the Georgian army. This group has been part of our multinational forces inside Iraq. He told me they were taking pictures of him because they said he looked just like them! I often wonder how many homes in Georgia have a picture of Rich up on the wall.

It took about ten days for Rich to adjust and get into a routine. He and a buddy began to work together with the Georgian army on their vehicles. They also helped train these guys in mechanics' work. Rich says they were so grateful for all the help, knowledge, and camaraderie established among them.

The guys at D-2 were taken on a tour of the historical sites inside Baghdad's Green Zone. I marveled at the CD that one of Rich's buddies had made for us. It's invaluable for us today because those tours are not allowed anymore. In fact, none of the men are allowed to take pictures of those sites today.

By August 23, 2005, Rich had settled down, and he felt they were now in one place and stabilized. He got assigned his own room, while most of the other men shared a room. I knew this helped him adjust easier. However, the bathrooms were outside (upstairs and outside). He explained it like, "Glorified outhouses and bathhouses all in one!" I was so glad we packed bath shoes for him. Our missionary experience proved helpful in packing for his Iraq deployment.

On August 26, 2005, I had to call the company's personnel department at Fayetteville, Georgia, to discuss benefits and salary. He had been gone for over three weeks, and his first paycheck hadn't shown up. I had also tried to fill his medications to send to him, with no luck. When I tried to use his benefit card, they told me he wasn't in the system.

It appeared that there had been a huge mix-up in Houston. The recruiter and the other personnel there had failed to send out the completed paperwork, according to HR stateside. A few guys were getting paid, but not everyone. The benefit package was also incorrect for Rich. All those papers we had filled out and sent in ahead of Houston appeared useless. We only had thirty days from his beginning date in Iraq to sign up for the correct benefit package.

One of the top HR managers in Fayetteville, Georgia,

  Linda J. Johnson

worked with me on this and got to the bottom of the problems for any of the men affected that had been in the same class as Rich in Houston. He took care of the issues and got back to me telling me they were profusely sorry for the breakdown in communications and that everything was now in place. I was so relieved.

Rich was called into the office by his site manager and literally chewed out because I had contacted HR in the States. He told me he just took it, while the other guys felt really bad for him. I called Fayetteville again and faxed them a three-page memo detailing what had been promised to us versus what had actually happened. I also asked them to tell the site manager in Iraq that the company had made legitimate mistakes and that they were being corrected by HR.

I also contacted the recruiter who had been in Houston. We had a long conversation about what was promised and what actually happened. I talked to him about the fact that we had never been told ahead of Rich entering Iraq that the airfare reimbursement for any leaves taken would only be reimbursed at $860. He replied, "Well, isn't he earning enough to cover that difference?" I reminded him that Rich would be flying home to Kauai from halfway around the world. We were all led to believe that the men would have fully paid round-trip tickets back and forth to Houston. After all, that's where they initially departed from. We knew that on any leaves Rich would schedule we would incur a cost round-trip from Houston. Needless to say, the rules changed!

This was just another twist to the new job. What could we do? Rich was already in Iraq, and they were already deducting $1,000 per paycheck. There was nothing we could do at that point. Rich would have to fulfill his contract so we could get our $5,000 reimbursed and continue toward financial recovery.

Meanwhile, Rich settled into his routine of twelve-hour days, seven days a week. He was issued his military ID and his orders. He was officially a U.S. Army contractor. He faxed his papers, his orders, and a copy of his military ID to me for me to add to his file.

Once again it appeared to me that it took a full two months for him to get organized. I was aware of the fact that we were both escalating up and down with our emotions. He was really gone, and I would just have to learn to live this way.

Our church clerk helped me a lot. Her husband had been deployed in the fall of 2004. She was able to give me valuable information about phone cards, shipping boxes, and rates, along with tips for staying occupied. She would also bring me meals occasionally, when she cooked for her family. I don't think she'll never know how grateful I was to her.

From the beginning of Rich's deployment, I was aware that there were no support groups for me. Military/army contractors and their families had and still have no support. We have no one to turn to. We have no place to go to when we need help. It was going to be a very, very lonely road.

CHAPTER 9

While Rich was bonding with his unit, I found myself alone and lonely. He began to make friends and establish some new relationships. It was uncanny for me to think about the fact that I wouldn't be a part of his new life. The fellowship on Kauai became my family, but no one could take his place. I spent many a night crying myself to sleep.

For the deployments of civilians during 2005 and 2006 and ahead of the surge, guys would actually get into a combat zone and immediately have to adjust to twelve-hour days for seven days a week, putting up with car bombings, gunfire, and air raid drills or calls to bunker. The stress of the adjustment to this environment would be ongoing for them and shared with complete strangers in most cases!

Another interesting part of this job deployment is that our men had to provide everything for themselves. They had to provide their own steel-toe boots and their own work clothing. We, the families, found ourselves faced with the daunting challenge of sending in whatever they needed whenever they needed it. In the early days at D-2, where Rich was stationed, facilities were few and options for finding anything were limited. It took six months or more for him to get set up. We have recently heard that there is a "test" group inside Iraq of military contractors who are wearing uniforms issued to them, which are a bit different than the regular military, but Rich has never seen them for the mechanics. He says the translators have them, however, and have had them since he was deployed.

When I think about it, I am so thankful and grateful for my Kauai and Hawaii extended family. These were our members and colleagues who were there for me if I expressed a need. They just weren't exactly sure how to approach me or whether they should intrude. It was a learning curve for all of us. To be fair to all of them, I didn't always ask for help or share how I was doing.

The fellowship was very busy for me, and it became my life (even more so than before). We had a service on Sunday mornings and at least one outreach cell-group meeting during the week, and two cell-group meetings every other week. These home meetings and Bible studies included sharing a meal and study along with prayer. Again, these were a great blessing to me and filled my time with positive interaction. Our people were anxious to be my "family" while Rich was deployed.

Communication, however, proved to be more difficult for Rich and me, because Rich has never been one to use a computer extensively. We began to schedule regular and longer phone conversations. That has been our main mode of communication while he has been in Iraq. We have tried to schedule a longer talk at least every forty-eight hours.

It was a great relief to me and gave me such a sense of peace when Rich got a cell phone with a direct line for me to be able to reach him. He had purchased the phone line from an army guy who was leaving Iraq. He had an international chip put in it, and I can still call him at any time (when I can get through).

The time difference has always been challenging. While we were on Kauai, he was twelve or thirteen hours advanced into the next day. I found myself living in three time zones—Kauai, the Midwest, and Iraq. There was only a small window of time those days where I didn't feel "on call," waiting for his calls or e-mails. I still feel that way, but we are only living in two time zones now! (He is plus nine hours from central time zone and plus eight hours during daylight savings time.)

I was very fortunate to have a good family friend from Kansas City, who called frequently during that first year of Richard's deployment. He was an air force retiree whom we had known since 1999. Ron would take my calls at any time. He fully understood the stress of an overseas deployment. (He was a veteran of WWII.) He and I had met as colleagues in the Justice Department in Kansas City during an assignment in 1999. He was a great encouragement to Rich and me to "stay the course." Most days he called just to ask how I was and what I had heard from Iraq. It was very thoughtful and meaningful to me to have that connection, most especially when I couldn't reach Rich.

After Rich had been in Iraq for about three weeks, he was told he could put in for his first leave. It appeared he would have to wait until January to come home, because so many guys were already scheduled. So we began to plan and look forward to that first reunion. We planned to bring our youngest son, Chris, and his children to Kauai at the same time. We now understand what the HR Department at Fayetteville meant when they told us that we should live from one leave to the next.

Rich began to share with me a lot about the guys he was deployed with. I reminded him that they should all try to become "one big, happy family" because all they would have was each other! There were former marines, navy, and army men in his unit. They had all been recruited due to their service background.

He told me about where they all had come from. They were from all over the U.S.A: Texas, New York, Florida, Kentucky, Illinois, Pennsylvania, California, and other states. I was so amazed.

We discussed the fact that almost all of them were married men and most had dependant children still at home. One big common denominator between these men was the fact that jobs had dried up back home for them, so they turned to the Iraq positions as a way of supporting their families.

Of course, almost all of them wanted to make a difference in this war and contribute to the effort. Rich and I also discussed that some may have been running from their problems back home, hoping that they would straighten out while they were in Iraq. We would discuss a lot about the fact that any problems the men had would follow them and would have to be dealt with by the group as a whole. It was a real eye opener for many of them. Rich proved to be an invaluable listener.

  Linda J. Johnson

I enjoyed hearing how they would discuss their families and the kind or size of home they lived in and what their hopes and dreams were for the future. They became each other's family because they were all they had.

More than once Rich would ask me to contact a family member back in the States for one of the guys and offer to help with advice or just hold a conversation.

Through Rich's early days in Iraq, I had lots of questions, and I was trying to understand the role of the LSI men in comparison to the military. Slowly I began to understand. These guys were filling a shortage for the MOS (military occupational specialty) of wheel mechanic for the army. There simply weren't enough mechanics to meet the needs of our military inside Iraq.

Rich explained early on that that some of the guys at D-2 were working for the Georgian Army, and the rest of them were working directly for the United States Army's front that was stationed at D-2/Prosperity Base. They were on multiple sites within the Green Zone during that time, but all housed together. Their jobs were to take care of the military's vehicles and insure that they were repaired and serviced and sent back into the field.

Rich enjoyed also the training aspect of the work. Oftentimes he was called upon to show the Georgians how to service their own vehicles, and they were very grateful. Even in the midst of all the chaos of daily bombings and sirens and an active war going on outside the walls, Rich adjusted and settled in for the long haul. The Georgian Army played a big support role to our military as part of coalition forces.

We talked quite often during those days on his cell

phone line, and I felt like I was also a part of his new life. It became clear that I would have to be available to him whenever he did call to talk because he needed to hear from me and know I was safe.

There were and are certain jobs that the army completes for their vehicles. These vehicles include humvees, trucks, and mraps. The company is contracted for everything else. The army is the client. But they work together, hand in hand, and a motor pool boss works with them. He is the liaison between the regular army and the LSI men.

I have fond memories of the first motor pool boss, Sergeant Harper, who got along really well with all the guys. I remember he was especially fond of chocolate macadamia nuts! He reminded Rich of that fact before both of Rich's leaves home to Kauai!

Rich had report, or a meeting, twice daily. Those were status meetings and updates. Everyone had to be present. When they were being moved in or out of Iraq, their meetings, or reports, could be even more frequent. (This is usually due to the fact that they are on a different base, and everyone has to be accounted for at all times.) Sometimes, during the daily briefings, they get news of what is going on around them (military news, or someone has heard what happened recently during incidents). Needless to say, the stories are much different than what we hear on the news here!

CHAPTER 10

I was also aware during those early days of Rich's departure that I couldn't spend a lot of time feeling sorry for myself. My family wasn't living anywhere close by, and it appeared to me that they didn't have a clue as to what was going on in Iraq. Support for our situation was limited, not unlike stories I had heard from our military families. Everyone seemed to have their own lives to live, and unless you were personally affected by a deployment, you didn't quite "get it."

Unfortunately, this was the case for my family. I didn't really feel during that first year on Kauai that I had their complete support when I needed it.

We lived far enough away that I couldn't get a posture on where they stood with this. None of them, other than our sons, ever came to Kauai to visit while we were there. I remember wishing for a visit from any of them, most especially after Rich left.

I would always be aware, though, that contractors in Iraq and Afghanistan don't have the support during our loved ones' deployments that the military has for their loved ones. One of the first encounters I had with the gap, or dividing line, between Rich's deployment and those in the active army or reserves/guards was when one of our fellowship wives on Kauai shared stories with me about her FRG (family readiness group). She received lots of support and help from the group, and wonderful camaraderie existed because of the commonality of the families deployed. They could call each other up and just knew what they were all going through together. For me there was *no one*.

When I was adjusting, I had no one to talk to who understood my frustrations and adjustments. Furthermore, I had to endure lots of comments like, "He's only there for the money, right? He's not really deployed. Isn't he *just* a civilian?" These comments to me were crass, crude, rude, and insulting.

Why didn't anyone understand that the same hardships of a deployment applied to contractors and their families just like the military? I was so frustrated and downtrodden and began to realize that our stories weren't out there. I wasn't even sure if our country knew or understood the dedication, sacrifice, and necessary work that our loved ones performed in Iraq. Certainly they didn't have the ability to understand that I needed more of their backup and support just to go on adjusting and supporting Rich while he was there.

It is just as tough for me to face another day without my husband as it is for a military wife. In fact, maybe it is tougher

Linda J. Johnson

because our men are placed in teams with guys they don't know ahead of deployment. Our families are never able to be introduced to each other or get a chance to bond and live near one another. We are in the same boat, but yet as families scattered across America, we don't get to know each other personally.

I didn't get to plan any gatherings to bring us together to help us cope and to discuss the unique problems we were facing with our loved ones in a combat zone. We didn't get phone calls of encouragement from LSI to tell us to "hang in there." I have found that in order to fill this role of support to my husband I have had to train myself as each new obstacle came along. I wasn't even sure how to explain my husband's position inside Iraq. It helped when I told people he was an army contractor, yet not military, but attached to the military and living on a military base.

The lack of events to attend regarding our loved ones' deployment or having no one to answer our questions whenever something happens that we can't get answers to are things we face alone far more often than military wives. They have other unit wives to turn to or liaison army personnel they can phone to get answers.

The communities that the military comes from stand behind their deployed units wholeheartedly and are always thinking up new ways to get behind the families left behind. This is the type of support that we need, and it only comes if we ask for it or point out to someone that we need it.

There isn't anyone knocking on my door when a water pipe bursts or when I am having problems figuring out how to change the fire alarm batteries! Rich and I have to have lots of these conversations while he is in Iraq and I am here, as I struggle to fix something on the homefront!

I think one of the most difficult aspects of Rich's service that I have found is defending his right to go work and serve honorably in this manner. From day one I've found myself educating the public about some of the things that our men do there and how vital I believe their role is.

The interconnection and co-working with the military is vital for a successful mission to be done in Iraq and Afghanistan. Our men fill in a job critical to keep the army's equipment running. They are contracted to do the very detailed and critical technical work on the vehicles. They are trained in and use military manuals. The following are some of the duties performed by my husband and the men on his team:

- Troubleshoot repairs and perform maintenance checks and services on military equipment
- Prepare vehicles and equipment for operation under abnormal conditions by sealing, waterproofing, and servicing with special fuel and lubricants
- Determine extent of corrective action and repair parts procedures
- Perform maintenance to correct malfunctions of mechanical, electrical, and hydraulic systems or components
- Perform troubleshooting and diagnostic repairs on military tactical equipment, ranging from small forklifts to HEMMIT fuel vehicles

Who else would do this work? It is highly technical as I mentioned and mission critical for our military.

  Linda J. Johnson

CHAPTER 11

On a lighter note, my longtime girlfriend, Charlotte, from Colorado Springs, made plans to come to Kauai in September of 2005, not long after Richard left, for the sole purpose of helping me get through the adjustment time. She wanted to be there for me and lend a hand with the fellowship as well.

This was her second visit while we lived there. However, this time she was a huge source of support to me personally! I'm not sure I would've gone through that early adjustment period as well as I did without this personal dear friend coming alongside me to show me that she understood where I was coming from in the unique situation that I found myself in.

I enjoyed her visit immensely. She is a morning person, and she would get up ahead of me and put the coffee on and just plan our day. She served as a motivator for me and a reminder that life had to go on as usual. We explored some of the sights on the island that I had never taken the time to see in the past.

She helped out with the fellowship and led some of our Bible study groups, giving me a short break and rest. She also helped me create a reasonable activity plan for the months of October through January. These were goals not only for me personally but for our fellowship. After I completed each goal, the idea was that it would be closer to January and Rich would be home for his first leave!

Charlotte has been a faithful and consistent support of both Rich and me throughout this entire deployment. She even included Chris while he was in Iraq. She regularly sends cards, notes, and boxes to Rich and Chris. This helps me immensely, knowing that they are getting mail if I have not sent anything during the week. She has been so helpful and generous. What a blessing to have her stand by our family.

Being a female, Charlotte understands the necessity of me needing a personal connection, and she has been the one who calls or phones remembering me just to see how I am doing. I can share anything with her and know it will stay with her. This is vital for me, as people oftentimes forget that I need support from somewhere. Her daily calls have helped keep me in touch with someone who supports us.

Charlotte is a sustainment architectural engineer for a major Defense Department contractor in Colorado Springs. She understands the relationship between civilians and the military, contracts, and the importance of the well-being of those personally deployed to a combat zone no matter what capacity they serve in. She knows how tough it is.

Charlotte can empathize with working in strange and

  Linda J. Johnson

remote places. She is an adult student graduate of our first state-side mission bridge school in 1991 in South Dakota. She first heard us speak of our overseas work back in 1989. She has been to the field with us in the Philippines twice and has supported our work for years. She has been an avid world traveler herself.

It would be hard for me to list all of the times I have been grateful to others, besides Charlotte, who have shared this burden with me. Sometimes I have only had to mention what Rich or Chris needed, and someone steps up to the plate to purchase and ship out a box or send a card to him or to me!

A lady from Ohio (Mary Jane Spees) has "adopted" Rich too. She also included Chris while he was there. Her goal has been to pick up a few deployed persons and write letters and notes to them to encourage them during their deployment.

I was able to finally speak with her on the telephone a while back and thank her personally for being such a help to me and an encouragement to Rich. Mail means so much to those guys. Just knowing that someone is thinking of them and writing to them is wonderful. She has oftentimes sent me the notes she includes to him, and they are always about her family and just routine daily stuff. Her husband is also a mechanic, so Rich feels connected to them now. We hope to one day meet all of them in Ohio.

When it came time for Charlotte to leave Kauai, I knew I wouldn't be seeing her for a while again. However, this time we had worked out some goals and a schedule that seemed reasonable to me. As I waved good-bye, I was encouraged that she would always be on the other side of the phone line whenever I needed her. And I would have someone that I could share with and who would accept whatever came my way with unconditional understanding and concern. Most importantly, as I saw her off at the airport, I realized that the next airplane I would welcome to the island would be bringing back my husband the following January!

In October of 2005, I flew to the mainland. This would be a two-week trip to Mississippi and Arizona. I was excited to have an invitation from the mother and daughter who we had helped through the drowning incident on Kauai. This visit was much needed to fill in some of the blanks for them surrounding that tragedy. I felt it was absolutely necessary to help them find closure.

I was also treated to Mississippi hospitality firsthand. It was an intense week, full of joys, sorrow, and healing.

We enjoyed a wonderful fellowship. In fact, the church they attended took on a project of sending goodies, candies, and treats out to Rich and his unit that Halloween season. I was so thankful.

After that, I flew to Arizona to spend a week with our Filipino godchildren. We hadn't seen them since 2004, ahead of our leaving for Kauai. This was a grand reunion and filled in some more time for me. When I got back to Kauai, it was already November!

CHAPTER 12

In November, Rich and I passed a few milestones. We celebrated our first wedding anniversary apart (our twenty-eighth), and he got a new roommate, so to speak! In the building next door to where Rich was housed, the military moved in Saddam Hussein. So, in essence, the former despot of Iraq was a neighbor. They kept him in that building because his trial was going on in there. Rich said there was lots of commotion regularly when Saddam was in residence.

In fact, during one phone conversation we were having early one morning in December, Rich informed me that he would have to go. A helicopter had just brought Saddam in and was unloading him not one-hundred feet away from Rich. He had been outside and upstairs by the helicopter pad to get a good signal to hear me. Suddenly he was in the middle of all the action! I asked him why he didn't get a picture, and he laughed at me. He asked me if I wanted to picture him getting wrestled to the ground by our own army!

Rich's first Christmas was approaching in Iraq. I panicked, wondering how I could make it special for him and the men in the unit. I wasn't sure I could do any better than I had already done for our anniversary. I had sent in a singing bear with a message, "Wild thing, you make my heart sing!" Everyone got a good laugh over that. Rich kept the bear on his toolbox. However, now I was concerned about Christmas.

I was busy getting our young people ready for their first Christmas presentation in over four years, but I knew I had to come up with something extra special for him in Iraq. Although we promised each other that we would celebrate Christmas later on in January, I knew that this wouldn't be good enough.

At the same time, Rich found himself in the process of a personal move. The building they were staying in was taken over completely by the army, and they were all going to move into hooches. The hooches had been brought in for their housing by the company that holds the contract. These were trailers with two sides and a bathroom in the middle. They are made to house one man on each side; however, up to four men are sometimes housed in them. At least they weren't the dry hooches that exist on many sites. Those trailers do not have a bathroom inside, and the men must go outside to a common restroom/shower facility.

Rich chose to room with Charlie and Terry. These were his marine buddies. Although I had never met them face to face, I would come to know them well through Rich. We shared some phone conversations and e-mails as well. Those guys were like the three musketeers! Rich and Charlie shared one side of the hooch, with Terri having the other. So they got a three-man trailer!

I was concerned for Rich because I knew how much he needed his rest at night. But he quickly adjusted to having another man in the room, and Charlie proved to be a good friend to Rich during the time he was there.

Although they proved to be polar opposites, they got along great. Rich is quiet and Charlie never stopped talking. I enjoyed hearing Charlie yell out, "Hello, Mrs. Johnson," whenever I phoned into Rich while he was in his quarters. This guy was a bright light occasionally in that place and kept things lively!

I did get to have some conversations with Charlie's wife during the course of his deployment. It was nice to talk to someone who understood what I was going through, and for a while we e-mailed back and forth. She told me that she had already been through this before, because this was Charlie's second deployment to Iraq since they had been married. But somehow this second time around was harder on her.

She had called to ask for some counsel and mentioned that Rich had been a great help to Charlie inside Iraq. We discussed the difficulties of marriage long distance, and I gave her some suggestions for keeping busy and then gave her the titles of some books on marriage that I would recommend. I also encouraged her to get involved with a good church fellowship in order to keep her mind lifted and her spirit strengthened.

We both laughed at some of the difficulties the guys were having and how they would ask for something right out of the blue and expect us to instantly get it to them in Iraq!

There was an instant bond between us, and she filled in some of the blanks for me concerning the parent company and the inner workings of contractors and the military since the earliest days inside Iraq.

It was so wonderful to meet, by phone, the wife of the roommate of my husband. We kept in contact until Charlie finally went home in December of 2007. Once in a while we still e-mail, and I hope to meet them in person when this is all over for all of us. Secretly, both Rich and I think that Charlie initiated our phone relationship. We are pretty sure that as he grew closer to Rich, he wanted his wife to have someone else to talk to on occasion.

I also tried to connect with some online groups of wives and girlfriends left behind; however, none of the groups were very uplifting or encouraging. A lot of the postings from those groups were more lightweight and frivolous to me. There was really nothing out there to unite us. None of us felt comfortable sharing our personal feelings with just anyone. After all, our husbands and loved ones were still in Iraq. It could compromise them, especially when we were told to avoid discussing their location or hometowns or any personal information that could get to the enemy of our mission. If someone shared "mission essential" information back then, when we were in the midst of heavy fighting, it could get back to their bosses or the military and they could face reprimand or write-ups. So many of the women were terrified for the safety of their husbands. A certain percentage of the women on these online sites had loved ones serving in security positions, and those men were targets because they worked "outside the wire," or off base.

One gal from Texas was helpful to me for about a year. Her husband was deployed with the largest contracting company in Iraq, and her son was deployed by the military. So, for a while we exchanged a lot of e-mails, along with phone calls. We lent quite a lot of support to each other.

She shared with me some ideas about what the guys really needed and what they would want over there, like their own pillows, sheets, or towels, and the best way to get them sent. She was always there to listen to me when I went through a hardship inside the fellowship or when I had family concerns. She stood in when I couldn't or wouldn't have the time to discuss and talk out issues with Rich due to where he was.

She was an excellent listener and had a calming effect on me. We discussed a lot of the news at the time, and it encouraged me to know she felt the same way I did regarding the omission of our loved ones from any reports or statistics about Iraq. She was a big help to me while I made the transition back to the mainland, encouraging me each step of the way and even helping me make some of the decisions for minor items inside the house we were building. She did all of this for me, yet she had four kids at home, along with a husband and a son deployed! She has been one of my unsung heroines!

I cannot emphasize enough how much the loneliness, isolation, and lack of support have been the hardest part of this entire experience. I always find myself in a position of defending the war, our military, and President Bush. Sometimes it is even harder explaining Rich's role there. No one really seems to understand or want to understand what our men do. We are really in the shadows of this conflict.

CHAPTER 13

Rich, in the meantime, passed the holiday season of 2005 in a non-festive fashion. He and the company men were never invited to the USO shows or any other celebration or parties. In fact, Christmas and New Year's Day were just more work days for them. He did tell me to watch Fox News channel because they had cameras in the mess hall, or DFAC, on Christmas Day. He thought maybe the cameras had turned toward him when they were interviewing some of the army guys! I never did see him on camera. The mess hall was decorated, though, and they had the traditional turkey dinner with all the fixings.

I reflected on the fact that Rich and the men he was deployed with would celebrate a major holiday and they had truly formed their own pseudo family.

This was rather like the military, with the difference being that our men had only just met each other in Houston for the first time. Therefore, besides having a personal adjustment of their own, they were adjusting to new people entirely, and furthermore, these people would be the "family" they shared the holiday season with. This was tough. We families back home were reliant upon the information that our loved ones told us concerning what was going on over there between the men.

He told me that they had put up the small Christmas tree I had sent to him for all of them to enjoy in the office. He also mentioned that all of the men appreciated the cards from our Sunday school kids and the hand-woven leis and other goodies sent to them from Kauai and Honolulu.

I had remembered seeing red, white, and blue leis given to some of our military in Hawaii. They had received these either coming or going to Iraq. I wanted to have some of those hand-woven leis for Rich's team. I called one of my co-pastor's wives in Honolulu and asked her if someone in her church would consider getting me three dozen of those done in time to ship for Christmas. She gladly accepted the challenge, and she told me they would get done. Gloria Bocobo came to my rescue once again. She had been so faithful in checking up on me by phone since the day Rich first left for Iraq, and she had personally comforted me at the Honolulu airport.

She committed to me that her church group would hand-weave those leis for Rich and his men for their first Christmas in Iraq. Later, I would find out that besides juggling a full-time job and helping her husband in the ministry, she alone completed all those leis! Their church actually sent in cards, goodies, and the leis as an encouragement to

Rich and his men. The guys immediately placed those leis on the end of their bunks as a good-luck charm!

My mom also called from South Dakota and said that her philanthropic sorority group in Mitchell was looking to sponsor service members or personnel in Iraq. She told them that Rich was there, and sure enough that group put together much-needed supplies of personal hygiene items like shampoos, conditioners, hand creams, toothpaste, and much more. Christmas 2005 turned out to be merrier than Rich had hoped, with all the support the men received from those dear people who mobilized for them to assist me to ensure their unit wasn't forgotten.

Rich told me how happy the members of the Georgian military were when Rich handed out some of the supplies for them to choose from. Those men were so very grateful because Rich noted that they received little or nothing from their home country. They were overwhelmed by the generosity and sharing by our men to them. Rich had also received a second small Christmas tree from one of the military support packages. He put this one up in his quarters. I was happy to know that they were okay there and that Christmas had been somewhat happy for them. They felt remembered.

I have been blessed throughout Rich's deployment to receive pictures and have communication from Rich's team of men. There would be no exception that Christmas. The guys took lots of pictures for me to see how excited they were to have been remembered by someone! This helped me to feel like a part of his life and a part of this conflict. We felt that we were both invested in the success of this endeavor.

Back on Kauai, I reflected on my first Christmas without Rich. We had spent many a Christmas in the past away from home or family, but never each other. I immersed myself in helping our church kids with their upcoming Christmas program and dinner. I had written the script, and we did a Scrooge-themed play. This was our fellowship's first Christmas program in four years, and the event brought lots of families together. We taped it for Rich and his men. They loved watching it later on.

As I was observing our kids during their presentation, I looked out over the ocean and wondered how many tears I had shed up to that moment since August. He would be home soon for a leave! I actually felt guilty sitting at that wonderful dinner and program at a beautiful resort hotel with warm Christian friends and colleagues while he was inside Baghdad. I couldn't wrap my mind around the depth of my emotions.

It's hard to explain also how it felt during those first months watching another couple walk together or what it was like to watch them at the movies together. I would sometimes just cry for no reason at all that first year. Whenever I took myself on a date to the movies, I would miss him. (Yes, I graduated to taking myself out to the movies alone for the first time in my life. It was a strange feeling.)

It was especially hard when I couldn't reach him by phone. Or we would be talking on a call, and the signal would drop or the call would get cut off. Sometimes we never reached each other back until the next day, or maybe even two days later!

Whenever an incident happened in the area near D-2, communications would shut down. This happened frequently in the first five months of Rich's deployment. I would call him and hear sirens and explosions, and then the signal would fail. It was mind-boggling and worrisome. I would have to wait for his call or an occasional e-mail to hear what was going on. Then they wouldn't always really know the full details. Communications are always shut down if there has been a death or multiple deaths of our service members in the area. This is so that families can be contacted before someone leaks the information. The communications were also interrupted in those early days whenever any incident happened nearby in order for the military to get their statements ready and ensure that no report of what had happened went out over the media that wasn't authorized.

CHAPTER 14

Before I knew it, it was the new year of 2006, and Rich and I had one thing to focus on. He was coming home for his first leave. I was so excited. I think I told everyone from the post office to the grocery store personnel. Maybe all of Kauai knew Rich was coming home on leave! It had been a long five months.

Chris and the kids were coming also, and it would be a grand reunion. Our members in the fellowship got gifts ready with leis woven and purchased to welcome them. Also, we kept up a Christmas tree for Rich and the grandkids to enjoy.

Chris's family would be there for five days of Rich's ten-day leave. We picked a hotel adjacent to our favorite beach, Lydgate Park. I could hardly fathom how awesome it was going to be. We wanted to have the little kids see the ocean and be reunited with their grandpa all at the same time!

My holiday season that year consisted of two days in

Honolulu and then back to Kauai for the grand New Year's festivities that the AhPuck family always hosted. There was lots of food, fireworks, and fellowship. It would truly be an exciting January, and I thanked God for getting us this far into our journey.

While I was getting ready for Rich's first leave, I couldn't contain myself. This was like having a second honeymoon! It was nice to plan menus again for the two of us. I cooked a large turkey for his homecoming, with all the trimmings! It would be so nice to have him *home*. It would be so nice to do "normal" things again as a married couple. I was ecstatic with anticipation!

The evening that Rich came off that plane was great. One of our members was there, working at the Kauai airport, and she greeted him with a traditional lei. Then he cleared the gates, and there he was! Jet lag hit him about six hours after his arrival. He had literally come halfway around the world to be home. It didn't seem to us that ten days would be nearly enough.

He slept and slept and would get up and move around for a few hours, and then he would sleep again! I knew what global travel was, and I felt so sorry for him, having to travel that far for such a short time. However, we weren't going to fuss about it!

The airfare for that first ticket was around $1,300, and the company would only reimburse $860. The reimbursement would be on a paycheck, after he got back into Iraq. Airline ticket prices have steadily increased, yet our reimbursement has not increased. There is no consideration given to us for the amount we have to pay over and above the $860. We often wonder about this. We purchased his airline ticket for his March 2008 leave, and it cost us $1,600. So, today, the costs have increased so significantly that for him to get home we are now paying about 55% of the cost for his tickets.

The summer 2008 leave that Rich completed cost us $1,090 out of pocket because his ticket price was $1,950 to Minneapolis from Dubai. We flew him into Minneapolis, instead of Sioux Falls and then used airline points to purchase a second ticket for $5 round-trip. This saved us about $200 on the quoted price to get him all the way home.

We have asked why there isn't an increase to the reimbursements, but we don't get a straight answer. This has proved to be a financial hardship for some of us. After all, they are not on regular pay when home. In fact, they are only allowed ten paid leave days, and if they take the maximum days allowed per leave (sixteen), four of the days are LWOP (leave without pay). Recently, a new rule has been implemented, and they must be back in Dubai on their last approved leave day, so we don't get that extra day home now. Their pay also doesn't restart until they get back *inside* Iraq.

One day I hope we get an answer as to whether the company is getting reimbursed for most of the ticket's cost *or* an explanation as to why the reimbursements haven't increased. Even the military receives cost-of-living increases, but not our men. We do not have an advocate in our corner on this issue either. The general attitude appears to be "take it or leave it."

An incident that happened during his summer 2008 leave also left us with a lot more questions regarding the reimbursement plan. Rich had already been transported from his site to the BTC on August 5, and was awaiting his out processing and schedule to leave for Dubai.

Then, on August 6, 2008, they got a message posted on the board at the BTC that all flights on the exact day he was scheduled to leave to Dubai would be cancelled. It appeared that Barack Obama's visit to Baghdad had shut down the airport, and many men and women were now scrambling to rearrange their flights and contact their loved ones to tell them they didn't know when they would get home.

Of course, Rich and I discussed how this had also complicated the return for many of those who were trying to get back into Iraq from their stateside leaves. They were stranded at Dubai and couldn't go forward into Iraq until the airport reopened.

I couldn't believe it. The company purchased Rich's new ticket at a $600 price increase, and Rich and I figured that at least one-thousand people or more were affected adversely by this. The company had to pay the difference because this was due to no fault of Rich's. Imagine the amount of money that was spent those few days to get our men in and out of Iraq just to accommodate a presidential candidate. The media didn't cover that story, and I wondered where the extra money came from all of a sudden to accommodate all those affected!

  Linda J. Johnson

CHAPTER 15

Rich first got to speak out about the subject of American contractors and his role in Iraq during a personal radio interview with Swarthmore College on his first leave in January of 2006. He not only wanted to clarify what he was doing in Iraq, but he didn't mind answering their questions as they were attempting to put a voice or two with their upcoming story.

The student reporters at *War News Radio* were doing a radio show about Americans working in Iraq. They interviewed Rich by telephone, and the show aired in March of 2006. They covered what motivates guys to go. They also covered what he was doing there, how he felt, and what he liked or disliked most about being gone from home.

I've always had to commend Swarthmore for being first with exploring this aspect of the conflict in Iraq. They were really on the cutting edge in understanding, or trying to understand, families like ours. The rest of the U.S. media wouldn't catch up to them until 2007. Even today, our families don't get the media exposure that the military does. There are really some distortions and misperceptions out there regarding a military/army contractor's role in Iraq.

It is important to let people know that not all contractors are earning much more money than our military while working inside Iraq. It is also important to us to share with America that some who have gone into a war zone are decent family men and women. They don't go to escape from problems or "get lost" inside Iraq. I think the biggest misperception is that many of our American contractors work unregulated or without supervision. This is simply untrue when it comes to military contractors. They have strict guidelines and rules that govern them on the job inside Iraq. It is also not true that any of our men or women are involved in harming or hurting the local Iraqi people. In fact, they form some very strong relationships with the local Iraqis they work with or with those TCNs who work in other capacities on base.

On Kauai, most everyone understood why Rich would go to Iraq, and they applauded him for it. Many of our own Filipino families had had experiences with their own loved ones having to work outside the Philippines as an OCW, or overseas contract worker, just to support their families back in the Philippines. Many Kauai vets had been approached by the Defense Department to go to Iraq as contract workers. It seemed like in Hawaii we were always hearing about someone who was inside Iraq working as a specialist for one company or another. They couldn't find positions back home in Hawaii that would pay them what they could earn working in Iraq.

  Linda J. Johnson

Of course, with all the politics of 2007–08, more and more stories surfaced. Yet most of the families were hesitant to be interviewed. It could cost their loved ones a job. The spin, however, on most of the stories was used against the war effort. They were published in an attempt to sway the public's opinion against war funding and/or President Bush.

Here is just one example of many articles that began surfacing throughout 2006 and appeared to be published for the main purpose of painting all contractors and employees inside Iraq who weren't active military as "bad people." I began to feel my stomach lurch every time another negative article or news story was published that seemed to portray any of our loved ones as less than honorable Americans.

The following is part of an article that appeared in November 2006. This is about the same time that positive stories had stopped coming out of the news media and the "tide had turned" with Americans openly criticizing the Iraq war in greater numbers and far more vocally than earlier on in the conflict.

> In the article "Contractors Rarely Held Responsible for Misdeeds Done in Iraq," written in November of 2006, the public is informed that contractors' misdeeds have increased substantially. The author, Griffe White, would have us believe that the companies are not held accountable whenever this occurs, due to legalities and lack of governing the companies. The reader is made to believe that Congress gives all of our contractors a "free pass" and looks the other way when it comes to any wrongdoings inside the Iraq war zone.

The critics of our American contractors, according to this article, cite lack of resources and personnel to do the oversight needed on the work that the companies contract, most especially for the work of reconstruction inside Iraq.

Stan Z. Soloway, President of the Professional Services Council, a trade organization of government contractors, defends their work, however, reminding the reader that they are performing within a combat zone and under extreme and changing conditions.

Scott Silliman, from the Center for Law, Ethics and National Security at Duke University, believes this is a difficult problem to solve because laws established in 2000 had never been tested as to the accountability for contractors in a war zone.[1]

The cost of this foolishness is a price we pay personally. We stay silent and quietly wait for our own family members to come home safely, with no fanfare and not much thanks.

Nonetheless, his first leave that January of 2006 was awesome. Chris and his kids' visit just added to our joyful reunion. Our fellowship really made them all feel welcome (Ohana-style).

One of our members loaned us a second vehicle so we could give Chris our car to drive while he was on the island. The grandkids loved the ocean and loved Hawaii, but most of all they loved seeing their grandpa! They still remember that vacation to this day and want to go back.

While Rich was home, he also saw the dentist and had labs drawn at the doctor's, as well as had an eye checkup. He had to get his flu shot too. It is always like that when he is home. He has to get appointments worked in for all maintenance meds and get his dental work done. He always has at least two appointments of some kind during every leave. It bothered me that they hadn't gotten the flu shots that were given out to the military that year. They always seem to be overlooked for those things.

At the present time, when he comes home for his leaves, we go through a checklist to see what he may need. He purchases it, and we ship boxes over for him ahead of his going back in (flat-rate U.S. post boxes).

Thank God for the U.S. Post Office and those flat-rate boxes. Without those, I don't know what we would do to send items in to him. I wouldn't want to guess at how many I've sent in to him since that August of 2005. I keep my own stock at the house with labels and shipping declaration forms. I never know when he will call for something, and I have to get it ready to go!

While living on Kauai, an island where everyone experiences having to purchase items and wait for shipments either from Honolulu or the mainland, I became a pro at learning which companies would ship directly in to him and save me double postage also.

At about the same time, after Chris's family left, Rich and I had a serious discussion about our own future. He was sure that he would be staying in Iraq longer than one year. He was just as determined as the rest of his team to stay a second year when it was already being offered to him and he wasn't sure about the employment situation in South Dakota, our home state. He had encountered limited job opportunities there in the past, and there was no army base on Kauai or in Sioux Falls that he could transfer to. He felt we were getting ahead financially and that he was excelling in his work. He asked me to consider buying a house and moving back to South Dakota. This would ensure that Rich would not have to worry about me, but would be able to stay with LSI and continue advancing his career.

We did a lot of soul-searching and made the decision to call a realtor friend of ours back in Sioux Falls. We explained our situation to him and told him it was probably time for us to move home to Sioux Falls. Wayne began looking at lots and developments for us. As I look back at how things unfolded, I am sure this was a most timely decision.

Wayne faxed us the information about a new subdivision northwest of the city. He thought that it would be the best location for us to buy and plan to build at. We began to nail down what we wanted to do and then promised to get back to him by e-mail and fax after Rich left. We would have to quickly decide on the timing of this move.

Looking back now, we are very happy to have made an offer and to have chosen the lot and house that we did. It was just the perfect timing for this market and for us. Our offer was accepted in February of 2006 via the Internet. We were on the way to finally moving back home. I would have family and friends to surround me while Rich continued on in Iraq.

We knew that there would be a lot of extra expense for us to make a move back to the mainland, so we began planning for an end-of-the-summer closing. We chose a modest home style and began to put the plans in place from Kauai.

It was a challenge, for sure, to do it by long distance. But it probably worked out better than we could have imagined. At least we weren't preoccupied every day checking on the builder

Linda J. Johnson

or the progress of the house. We couldn't since we were too far away. I would send everything presented to me to Rich via the Internet, and then he would get back to me, and I would get back to South Dakota. It was quite the process!

Rich instructed me to begin with the $5,000 reimbursement money the company had kept from him until after he completed his first six months of service. After that, I was adding $1,000 per paycheck towards the down payment. We were very fortunate in that our previously-owned duplex at Kansas City also sold that February. We got that outstanding home loan and obligation out of the way.

Just the thought of planning a move, building a home long distance, and managing our fellowship was enough to throw me into major stress. If that wasn't enough for me to begin to comprehend, I realized that all of this would have to go on while I was backing Rich up constantly and daily, while he was inside Iraq. It was mind-boggling to me, and on every phone call during those months after he left, he reminded me that I could do it.

All of this was placed upon my shoulders because Rich was gone. It was a lot of stress during the time from February to May. Rich planned to be home for another short leave the end of May, and he would say some of his good-byes then. We would be able to finalize some things at that time, and he could help me out some.

We would also have to plan and make a decision for the timing of his leave at the end of his contract year, August of 2006. He would be eligible for a twenty-one-day leave, and he wanted to spend it in his new house! If I could accomplish all of this successfully, we would enjoy our own home and be fully moved in during that leave.

It was now a bittersweet time for me, planning for a new home yet knowing at the same time that we would be leaving behind our people and the beautiful island of Kauai. I tried not to think about it too much. There wasn't a moment to spare for me for all of 2006. That year flew by. This helped so much to pass the time and fill in the days without Rich around.

While Rich got back safely into Iraq, in February of 2006, the weather on Kauai took a turn for the worse. It started to rain, and the heavens opened up with no let-up! This caused all of the people on Kauai to get skittish and feel confined. The days were so gray! The coastal waters turned brown, and each night brought the pounding of rain on the rooftops.

Oftentimes during that timeframe, I would hold the phone up to the window, and Rich could actually hear the rain pounding on the ceiling! That was through the phone all the way to Iraq.

Then Kauai experienced tragedy. A raging wall of water broke loose from a reservoir near Kilauea, north of Lihue. It washed out land and homes on its rush toward the ocean. It also washed out some of the main highway connecting the North Shore to the main county seat of Lihue. Seven people lost their lives that day, and some of the bodies were never found.

It was an ominous event for all of us locals. Everyone speculated as to what was happening. I just remember enduring about seven weeks of rain. Day after day, beaches were closed, and people were not allowed into the water. Those were dark days on Kauai. For me it helped to confirm that our decision to leave was right on. Without family there, it was hard to experience those days and that darkness of attitude.

CHAPTER 16

On March 22, 2006, I received a box from Rich full of gifts for me! He had some rugs, wall hangings, and T-shirts inside. One of my favorite T-shirts that he sent had the OIF logo on front, and on the back was written "Who's your Baghdaddy?" I put it on right out of the box because I was missing him so much. This box seemed to be a connection to him. I went off to my aerobics class very happy, wearing the T-shirt.

After class, on that dark and rainy day, I stopped over at the post office to get the mail. While I was there, a horrible and frightening incident occurred. A woman came up behind me and said, "That is one stupid (and then she used a curse word) T-shirt."

At first I couldn't believe my ears, but then she said it again. This time she also stepped in front of me. She began a verbal assault on me, our president, and our troops, and she was trying to actually start a physical fight! I calmly asked her, "Have you ever met a real Iraqi person?" I assured her that our men were not killing innocent civilians.

I knew this due to the fact that our men aren't even armed and they don't interact with local civilians inside Iraq unless they are working with them or the resident Iraqis are cleared to be on base. Nonetheless, no one in my husband's job category is carrying weapons or doing anything other than working together for the mutual benefit of and services to our military.

It was useless. She had her mind made up. She chose to be abusive and make a scene in the public post office spewing her own misguided political views. She was screaming and shouting continuous obscenities as I made my way to my Jeep. I told her at one point, "I feel sorry for you" (because I actually did, in a way, for making such a fool out of herself in a public place).

As I hurried to unlock my vehicle and escape the abuse, she yelled, "Get (and she used another curse word) out of Hawaii. We don't want your kind here." I was so shocked that I called up my music minister and asked him to give me the non-emergency number to the police department. He gave it to me and told me to start home, but not to go home. He would drive my direction and meet me halfway if I was that afraid. He didn't want anyone following me to where I actually lived.

I reached the police dispatcher and told her what had happened. Her first question was, "Was she a *haole*, white person?" to which I replied, "Yes." A lot of what goes on in Kauai has a racial connotation of one kind or another. It is a much-divided place, and locals battle it out for territory. Everyone is a minority in Hawaii. There isn't one ethnic

  Linda J. Johnson

group that is more numerous than another, so therefore the dispatcher was attempting to figure out how to handle the incident just based upon just who was involved!

Then the dispatcher told me that she was glad I hadn't physically reacted, to which I was floored again! I gave her the license plate number of the truck the gal had climbed into, and she recorded it. She said she would be sending a police officer over to my house to get all the details.

I was so shook up, shocked, and actually very afraid after that encounter. I cried when I got home and wished I could've reached Rich, but I would have to wait. It was the middle of the night in Iraq, and he would be asleep.

By the time the policeman arrived, I calmly relayed to him what had happened. He said it shouldn't have happened, but I should "understand" that some people are against the Iraq conflict. Then he suggested that I refrain from wearing the T-shirt in public in the future. I told him I would not do that, just because my rights to freedom of expression (in wearing a T-shirt sent from my husband) were being infringed upon. I also reminded him that I have to view offensive clothing on people many times, and I just look the other way but don't confront them, intending to fight! Then I reminded him that she was actually threatening to me and that this was a small island. I wanted to know who she was and where she lived for my own personal safety.

He explained to me that they would find the gal and warn her. It was against the law to accost someone in a federal building or make threats against another person due to new Homeland Security rules. He also planned to talk to the post office personnel and ask if they recalled the incident. I told him there were lots of people who witnessed the incident but didn't want to get involved.

The local police never got back to me. After that, even when I called to find out who I should be concerned about, they told me it was taken care of. So I gave the truck description and license plate number to the family I lived with and to our fellowship. We were all on the watch for this vehicle for the next couple of months. I never saw that woman anywhere on the island again. However, I felt vulnerable, not supported, and very, very alone! I knew that if the same incident had happened to one of our members or their family, it would have been straightened out immediately.

Later on the day of the incident, I reached Rich and told him about it. He was so angry, and he felt helpless to comfort me from so far away. We both knew right then that the time couldn't arrive soon enough for us to leave Kauai. He no longer felt comfortable with me all the way over in the Hawaiian Islands while he was in Iraq. He wanted me "home" in South Dakota. The last thing he needed was to have to worry about me being safe. He was dealing with enough issues regarding his own personal safety there. Charlie did offer to fly on over and take care of the situation post haste! I laughed when I imagined those guys ever getting off a plane on Kauai and "taking care of business"!

Imagine my surprise, as I was e-mailing my family about what had happened to me inside the post office, that I got a less than supportive response. I wouldn't have thought that it would start a debate within my own family. One of my family members though was e-mailing me comments that were anti-war, anti-corporations, and anti-President Bush. Instead

  Linda J. Johnson

of understanding how traumatic that incident had been to me and how I could not understand the lack of support that some people were displaying, he actually agreed with the woman. He asked just why and how Rich could continue to work inside Iraq when our own military was committing acts of violence against innocent civilians. I was shocked at his negative attitude, when I fully expected support, not political rhetoric. He told me that he was only concerned for Rich, to which I responded, "If you are so concerned, then how many cards, letters, or packages have you sent him?" My own family was polarized during that time and playing politics at the expense of Rich and me. It was heartbreaking.

Instead of expecting any future support or understanding from many in my family, I kept busy working on details for the building of our house and preparing our people for my departure.

Fortunately, I received a phone call during this time, and a very close family friend committed to me that she would take vacation time from work to come out in the future at the time of my impending move, and she would help with everything. She told me to basically forget about the incident and move on and concentrate on the busy schedule of the coming months! It was good advice.

CHAPTER 17

As Rich and I put that experience behind us, he was happy to report that spring that he had gotten a raise! They were told their uplift was being increased because the army had increased theirs. So a portion of that uplift was given to our men.

Most Americans have a misperception or misunderstanding of the military contractor's role. Our men actually work on the front lines, inside the wire, directly with the army. Their wages are comparable to a staff sergeant's pay of $80,000 for twelve months, if that staff sergeant is deployed to a combat zone.

Any time off for our loved ones is reimbursed at base pay only. Holidays taken are on base, mostly spent in their hooches or housing units, and paid at eight hours. In addition, their benefits will not continue after Iraq. Many of them haven't seen active military duty and will have no follow-up support after Iraq and no guarantee of a job.

When they quit contract inside Iraq, they are done for the most part. They have to reapply for the same positions or similar positions stateside. Those positions are on army bases and depend upon current demand. Therefore, this affects their stress levels on the job, and they are always aware that they and their families are living from paycheck to paycheck and that contracting work is uncertain.

We do know that there are those who receive higher pay or six-figure incomes inside Iraq, working for the company. These people are oftentimes in administration or management. The guys working hand in hand with our military, like Rich, aren't making an inflated salary. Instead, our men are sacrificing home and family to have steady work. Many of them, like Rich, actually feel proud to be contributing in this manner to the effort there.

Both Rich and I have another bone of contention with the company regarding their sleeping arrangements. The company doesn't see to it that the mechanics get their own sleeping quarters. In fact, at D-2, only the site manager has his own quarters, and everyone else is now doubled up. Although Rich has held all but the site manager position, he had to share quarters with the administrator in the past and with other mechanics. Imagine four, or even three, grown men in the two sides of a small trailer or hooch, all having to share one bathroom and put in the hours they do.

Also, they get tired of being together twenty-four seven and then cannot even get a break on their downtime. Apparently the company holding the contract won't bring in more living quarters for our teams. However, other contracting company American employees don't usually have to double up. I have heard from wives who state emphatically that their husbands wouldn't hear of sharing their living quarters.

There are certain times when everyone shares rooms, regardless of whom they work for, when being transported to and from their personal leaves. It's a shame to put that extra burden upon our men. These mechanics, who work on the front lines, are treated with fewer amenities than management personnel within the company. It doesn't make any sense. The mechanics already sacrifice every day and make do with what they can. Management and administration, on the other hand, keep growing in numbers and handing themselves raises and special perks within Iraq. I really wish our men could've been organized as a union for these jobs.

With Rich, even though he has been stable and based on the same site since August of 2005, he has had to move his personal belongings five times. He has done this in order to attempt to have alone time and a room without a roommate. Every time he moves, his body wears down, and he gets a cold. So far he has been alone in his quarters for twenty-four months and has spent twelve months with a roommate. The company keeps bringing in more men to D-2, but gives them no more sleeping units! Go figure.

Fortunately for Rich, he knew his last roommate quite well. It was James (name changed), the administrator. They had been together since Rich began on-site there. So, they both knew the drill, and they had been through a lot together. Rich could trust him and manage to get along during that few months they shared a bunk room.

I get so tired of hearing all the negative comments from the public like, "Isn't he *just* a civilian?" as if that made a difference to his level of stress or to the work he provides to our military in a combat zone. Another frequent statement made in front of me is, "All contractors are profiteers, and the American public is wasting money inside Iraq." In general, there is so much ignorance about our loved ones and just who they are or what they do. There is also a lot of ignorance regarding the fact that military contractors work with and for the most part are very compatible with the military they serve. It wouldn't work any other way for any of them. Rich always tells me when a new army unit or battalion comes in it just takes time for the men to get to know what he and his guys do and then it becomes a compatible environment very quickly for the good of the mission.

  Linda J. Johnson

CHAPTER 18

During March of 2006, I flew to Fresno, California, to Patten University for a post-graduate course and studies for certification as a community services chaplain. The emphasis on this course would be CISD (critical incident stress debriefing). This was a thorough and very necessary course for me to take in preparation for the future. Rich and I both felt that I could benefit much on Kauai from taking this post-graduate course, and I would be able to utilize the certification for the future back in South Dakota. I felt that I would be able to help with families who had loved ones return to the States after deployment, whether they were activated as military units or contractors. I sensed that the need for trained people would be great in the future, and I would want to help.

There were over thirty adult students studying that credited course. There were also some undergraduates from campus who joined us for several sessions. It was an intense experience for me, as well as a refreshing time with colleagues from our denomination. I made some lifelong friends there. The course covered such topics as acute stress syndrome, delayed stress syndrome and cumulative stress syndrome. We discussed and studied counseling in the workplace, depression in the workplace and sensitivity, along with diversity. Grief counseling and suicide counseling were included, along with death notifications. All aspects of the chaplain as a counselor were studied and role playing was used extensively to support the studies.

The most interesting portion of the entire course to me was the critical incident stress debriefing portion. At the end of the course, after we passed our exam, we would be certified to work within communities to debrief first responders at the scene of large scale tragedies. This certification would also allow us to sit down with individuals and help them deal with traumatic experiences or incidents that they needed to "talk out" with a professional. The community service chaplain works mainly outside the walls of a church or building and works with the populace wherever there is a need.

When I was able to reach Rich from Fresno, the signal was clearer than it had ever been on Kauai. It seemed as if he was right next door! I was trying to give him a daily review of what we were covering and tell him about some of the people I had met, and it was thoroughly enjoyable that our conversations were without the usual static. My studies kept me quite busy and challenged while there. I looked at the experience as another fully scheduled segment of time filled in until Rich's next R and R!

  Linda J. Johnson

He was scheduled to be back in May of 2006 to help pack boxes and ship his toolbox to the States. Meanwhile, I was scheduled to leave Kauai on July 27. I was able to use his accumulated airline points to secure a free ticket back home.

As I look back on that spring of 2006, I often wonder how I went day by day without my soul mate there. I had to make so many decisions without him. Then I had to try to remember what all I had accomplished so I could relay it to him. This took some planning too, because there were some things better left unsaid. I wanted to be sure that I was giving him all the information and updates he needed but made sure I didn't give him too much to worry about. It was a delicate juggling act.

The men were in an especially volatile time in Baghdad right then. There were car bombings almost daily and constant incidents. The way Rich described it, those days came and went for him like something out of an apocalyptic movie.

To further keep myself occupied, I had volunteered to be the first "teen court" chaplain for Kauai. The teen court program was developed there and was quite effective for the community. The teen court program on Kauai gave young people under the age of eighteen a chance to work through their first offenses without incurring anything negative on their permanent records. Kauai Teen Court was a diversion program for first-time juvenile offenders. The program was voluntary, and even though the setting was less formal than family court, the same rules of confidentiality, promptness, and respect for the process applied.

The program is based on restorative justice and the ability of the offender to make things right, instead of punishment.

One of the primary goals of that teen court was to build skills, promote competency, and leave the respondent with new choices, which would hopefully prevent re-offenses.

Participation in Kauai's program required that the juvenile plead guilty as charged. Then he or she attended an intake session with one or both parents present, and a hearing date was assigned. Their hearing was held before a jury of teens, some volunteers, some former juveniles, and a court clerk.

Sentencing elements included community service, serving as a teen court juror, mandatory attendance at skill-building classes, or getting counseling and having to write letters of apology to victims.

My role was to help the kids with their apology letters and counsel them during their time of service required. I was also asked in some instances to set up counseling with the parents of the offenders. It was a rewarding experience, and I saw kids change before my eyes.

Once again I encountered the deep, dividing lines of racial barriers, as seen through the eyes of the kids that came into the program. When I could, I hope that I helped them see another side to *haoles*, or whites/Caucasians, and our culture. I believe I understood them in a way that was different from the other adult volunteers due to our missionary background and experience working overseas. We knew also what it was to experience prejudice directed at us personally. It was rewarding for me to encourage a wayward kid and motivate them to want to choose wisely in the future, as well as help them to get rid of some of their familial attitudes that ultimately worked against them.

I received a phone call in April of 2006 informing us

  Linda J. Johnson

that Rich's uncle had died back in Pipestone, Minnesota. We asked Chris to go there for the funeral to represent the family. He went up and stayed at Rich's oldest sister's home. After the funeral, while he was headed back to Kansas City, I told him to stop over in Sioux Falls.

He had no idea until that day when he called me from our lot that he was the first one from the family to step foot upon our property and view the progress of our house! He said he liked the area and that the homes being built were impressive. He was happy for us. He did say that only the basement was poured and that there were no walls up yet!

From that point on, we were to begin a series of discussions and confrontations with our builder and his crew via long-distance phone calls. Our closing had been scheduled for August 31 or before, and this was April, with not much progress. I got frantic!

Rich came home in May, and we knew it would be his last visit to Kauai. He and I picked the inside paint color for the interior walls of the house, and he had some conference calls with our builder's production manager, along with our realtor.

I noticed that I hadn't gotten upset during that second leave when Rich kept his travel bags packed and on the bed in the spare room. I was really proud of myself. He never really fully unpacked. This had bothered me so much during his first leave, but now I realized that he had to do this because he was living there, not here! He was just keeping himself organized.

We also gave notice to the family hosting us. They formally told Rich good-bye. They also assured us that they would do the same thing if they were in our situation. We are anxiously awaiting their visit here one day to South Dakota!

Rich also insisted upon taking our music minister to lunch during his leave. Our music minister was in total agreement with Rich's decision also. He told him, "If it was my wife, I would move her to be near family also."

We agonized over the fact that our people would be shaken up, so we decided not to have a meeting with them. We wanted to wait until Father's Day to make the announcement. On that Sunday, their former pastor would be visiting, and we felt this would help cushion the blow. Our district supervisor was in full agreement with this plan, and they promised to lend a hand where I needed it. It appeared that there was so much to do and so little time.

Rich packed up and shipped his tools to South Dakota. This was one last thing I wanted him to do. He and I also got one shipment of boxes ready to go to Sioux Falls, to be stored at a friend's house. That leave, for us, was a working and reconnecting time all in one. We picked out suitable dates for his leave for the end of the contract at the end of the summer. Our goal was on target for me to be in the new house and have it ready for his twenty-one-day leave.

We also were able to reserve a landline phone number and service for Internet and cable at the new house ahead of time. This was very important for Rich to put into the system for contact numbers when the time came. We really felt like we had accomplished a lot during his time at home.

  Linda J. Johnson

CHAPTER 19

Our son Chris, in the meantime, had been in the application process with Rich's company to go to Iraq as a mechanic like his dad. His dad had put in a good word for him, and Chris was waiting for a deployment date. Chris and I had worked out his contract papers and had gotten his passport renewed, so he was on hold with the company. Chris is a separated army vet who had enlisted in Kansas Army Reserve back in 1999. They had sent him home after basic training due to a knee injury from high school soccer. However, his separation has qualified him for OSGLI (service members' life insurance) and possibly some other military benefits. Chris preferred to deploy with this military contractor, however, because he wanted to spend the time there with his dad. He would also be able to receive military credit on his permanent record for the time being served as a military contractor in a war zone.

None of the problems that his dad encountered made a difference to Chris. He wanted to be there and do his part for our country, and he felt he needed to get out of Kansas City. We were fully supportive of his decision believing that he would finally find something to sink his teeth into and possibly re-enlist with the military due to this exposure and experiences. We believed that an LSI position would give Chris focus again and restore some of his self-esteem.

I was so proud of Rich's role inside Iraq at that point that I believed Chris could find his niche also. It gave me a comfort to know that they would be together in there.

Rich and Chris spent a lot of time on the phone discussing the probability of that happening and what Chris should expect when the company called him. There had been a halt put on deployments for the summer of 2006. We believe the company was awaiting the funding and the Defense Department's decisions before they deployed more men.

Rich did get a commitment from his site manager at D-2 that whenever Chris was in Houston, the site manager would put in for Chris to be placed at D-2. We were all relieved.

Chris was going through an exhausting and emotionally draining divorce. His now estranged wife was asking for child support to the tune of $1,900 monthly. Apparently she and her attorney had the same idea as the media and half the country at that time about military contractors. They appeared to view them as "cash cows." The war in Iraq had become such a polarizing issue by that time, and so many anti-war activists and some politicians were beginning to convince the public that every man who deployed as a contractor made bloated salaries and was unnecessary or frivolous.

  Linda J. Johnson

We got to laughing about it later, because at that time, Chris was lucky to have $19 to his name at any one time! He needed to get out of Kansas City and get his head on straight. We prayed for the best for him. Chris could always count on his dad and me to discuss these issues with him and encourage him to stretch at a time when he maybe would've given up on himself.

We were both busy a few days before Rich's departure copying all his orders and other documents, which he was always required to carry. I keep all his documents and copies of his passport and driver's license and contact names in a special file. I always refer to that whenever I need something. We have his airline ticket records back to his first leave, along with his requests. We have all of his performance reviews, copies of his updated résumé, and official letters from the company. It's very important to keep those things in one place and easy to access.

As Rich and I spent our last day together overlooking the Pacific Ocean, we both prayed for the strength, wisdom, and courage we would need to make this transition back home. We couldn't yet see that he would not be able to come back permanently from Iraq, though, as soon as we had planned. He was concerned for me to have to take care of so many things, and I was worried because I knew he was going back into a very dangerous place that was so unstable. He was good at hiding any dread he may have had. I tried not to tell him all of my worries.

Rich has been my confidante and best friend for so long. Living without him had left an empty hole in my life. Sometimes I miss him so much that it actually physically hurts. I no longer reach across the bed at night or when I wake up expecting him there. It appears like a resolve to me that he won't be there. However, that just makes each leave more precious. We cherish the time together now and realize how much each minute together counts.

It's funny, but in the evening, around news time, I will glance at the clock, no matter where I am, and remember that he is only beginning his day, and I am ending mine! In the morning I wait for his call, if it is a longer pre-scheduled phone call. I will then plan the rest of my day while he is going back to the bunk to sleep. I have an eight to ten-hour window each day when I know he is sleeping. I know I shouldn't ring him then, and I can get whatever I have to do out of the way.

When I know he is sleeping, I try not to disturb him. That action was very important when he was sharing quarters, and I did not want to disturb someone else. However, if I do ring his phone, he is gracious to listen to me and never gets annoyed. (Then he falls back asleep.)

During his leaves, I try to keep his home time balanced between friends visiting, some family time, and necessary appointments. Of course, upon arrival, he needs lots of rest, and I always expect that. He is so tired and has to get through jet lag and unwind and finally adjust to being home. Then, forty-eight hours ahead of his departure back to Iraq, we are on alert again. He becomes jumpy and nervous and doesn't relax until he boards that flight. It causes such a whirlwind of emotions. There is nothing to describe it. It appears that I lose him all over again.

We have been thankful that we are older and expect to be

  Linda J. Johnson

able to handle this. I cannot imagine the younger couples or those with children in the home! It is so hard being up and down; you have to concentrate on your long-range goals in order to live like this.

One of our members on Kauai, a special friend of mine, Nora Juan, spent two days ahead of his leaving, baking goodies for him to take back to the guys. We were so excited for him to be able to get those there for the men to enjoy. We had taken her into our confidence about his leaving, and she wanted to send him off with a special package for the team. She realized that it might be a long time before she got to see Rich again due to our upcoming move from Kauai. She wanted to do this as a gesture of *aloha* once again from Hawaii.

Rich had spent a lot of time on that leave discussing the food situation inside Iraq. Rich has always told me that there is always enough food available to them. It was just that it had all begun to taste the same! This was especially true by three years into his deployment. He was very sick of the same taste and thought it was the oils they used.

When Rich and I reached his gate at American Airlines, the security personnel and Agriculture Department almost confiscated those baked goods. Then the copilot came through the gate and told them to let Rich take those items. He told the agricultural people, "Mr. Johnson is taking those to some very tired, hardworking, and grateful men." We were so relieved.

Rich later told us that when he got those baked goods into Iraq, it took only one meeting for the men to devour them all! They sent a thank-you postcard back to Nora. She was so proud to have done her part to bless those guys.

On Kauai, I now found myself living in those three time

zones more than ever. It seemed as if I didn't get much sleep at all. With all the phone calls and e-mails back and forth to the mainland, the time flew by. There was so much action going on in Iraq, in the meantime, that I could expect e-mails or phone calls from Rich either early morning or late at night. There was only a small segment of time that remained in any twenty-four-hour period for me to have to myself, possibly six hours maximum.

  Linda J. Johnson

CHAPTER 20

On June 8, 2006, I flew to Seattle with one of our Filipino families. We were going to attend the college graduation of Nora's daughter. This would be the first college graduate in their extended family. It was a delightful experience.

On June 12, right before we were to leave Seattle, I was talking to Rich on the phone. He told me that President Bush had just left the IZ/Green Zone.

I remember telling him, "No, honey, President Bush isn't *in* Iraq; he is at Camp David meeting about Iraq."

He laughed at me and said, "Just wait until you get back to Kauai and read the morning's newspapers; the press will have the story by then. He was really just here."

Sure enough, on June 13, the story broke in the U.S.A., and President Bush had kept that visit a secret. Rich knew all about it because the detail surrounding the president caused the gates to be closed there at D-2, and some of the men were stuck off site until the president got back in the air to leave for America!

It was then that I realized how very important Rich's position was and that the men were in a most strategic spot there at D-2. They were right in the thick of things happening in Iraq.

Back on Kauai, as I discussed our leaving further with Nora, she was devastated, as was I. I didn't want this to be such a shock for her. I wanted her to have time to digest this. She understood and offered to help me in any way possible. Her family became our main source of help for me to complete the necessary preparations to leave Kauai.

The upcoming move scheduled now for July 27 occupied a lot of my thinking and downtime. I had to keep assuring myself that this was the right thing for us to do and that it would all work out for the best. I realized that one very important aspect about being back in the Midwest was that I would be closer to family and longtime friends. Another nice thing about moving back to the mainland for me would be the ability to finally segment my days into two time zones instead of three!

Eventually I knew I would be able to just be in central and Iraqi time zones. This would give me more time in between when Rich would go to sleep or wake up. I have always counted that space of time as my own or free time! While Rich and Chris were both deployed and on two different bases, my downtime, when I wasn't on call, was reduced dramatically.

My move back to South Dakota went relatively smooth. I had long, long days and some sleepless nights. There was so much to do, and without Terri there, I don't think I would have been able to accomplish it. She had been a close family

  Linda J. Johnson

friend from South Dakota since 1981. We had first met on a trip to Israel. I was very glad to have her back on Kauai for a second time helping me with all the physical aspects of the move. She also got to take a break and have vacation time away from her demanding job as a nurse in a nursing home.

We had to finish selling furniture, hold a rummage sale, pack and ship the last of the boxes, and clean up the flat left behind. It was an enormous task, and all without Rich there to help me.

Later on, Terri told me it was one of the most challenging experiences of her adult life! I really wasn't supposed to lift anything, and she had to do a lot of the physical work. She kept me as calm and as focused as possible during that hectic time.

Nora was also true to her word, and in between working two jobs, she allowed us to hold the rummage sale at her home. She later stored everything that hadn't been sold at her home. Rich and I were so grateful to the Juan family. Nora even loaned me her second car after mine sold. This was all a great help to me in the transition.

Looking back, I cannot believe that Rich and I purchased a vehicle, built a house, and moved our household back to the mainland by spending lots of time on the telephone and e-mail! Without this modern technology available to us, we would not have been able to do this. When I mention to others what we did in purchasing a lot and building a house long distance, people are amazed. They tell me it took great courage for us to do this. I tell them that it took a lot of coordination of details from Kauai to Iraq and back to South Dakota.

Rich was able to seal the deal for our vehicle and use his corporate discount to purchase a Ford Escape. He and our salesman back in Sioux Falls worked out the timeframe and details while Rich was on his May leave. It worked out okay long distance because we accepted the vehicle suggestion from the dealer for one they already had on the lot.

Sometimes I think it all happened like a constant dream unfolding over a six-month timeframe!

All of this was done in good faith. Our realtor and Terri had been taking photos all along of the building progress, so we were able to have those in front of us while making decisions.

We were successful in getting the closing date moved up to August 15, 2006, so I could be in the house and get it ready for Rich to come in on August 28. He would get his three weeks home in his new house!

During my last weeks on Kauai, I encountered more stress and overcame more physical health trials than I had in a very long time. I'm sure that taking care of all of these things made me stronger and served as preparation for the long days ahead of being alone. My migraine headaches came back with a vengeance, and I couldn't seem to get the lower back pain under control. I was wearing a back brace for most of those weeks.

As I discussed on the phone what was happening to me, which included extreme anxiety, along with pain and fatigue, my close friend in Honolulu, Gloria, again came to my rescue. She realized that I probably wouldn't ever take a break and that I needed immediate help. She was determined to come over to Kauai to help take some of the stress off of me, to give me some much needed downtime, and to be there as a confidante. She offered to pick up some of the slack wherever she could.

I asked her to speak to our fellowship and help me to help our people with the idea that transition and change

  Linda J. Johnson

was coming to them and that it was just as hard on me as it was on them. We would all be saying good-bye, and we had bonded together closely during our stay there. They were my "family" since Rich had left.

During the visit, she also assured our people that their own fellowship in Honolulu would be there for all of them after I left. This was a selfless gesture on her part, and I loved the few days we had to just unwind.

The speed with which everything happened was also difficult for me. I was actually dreading leaving Kauai and the people behind and would count down the days because the change for me was going to be traumatic as well. I didn't know if I could get used to South Dakota again or if I would even want to be there. I didn't know what I would be doing in addition to being the backup to Rich and Chris, and part of my own identity was being lost. I didn't know how long my adjustment would take to get used to another new place again.

As scheduled, we left Hawaii on July 27 and arrived in South Dakota on the 28. When I look back, I am so thankful that the TSA (Transportation Security Administration) hadn't yet implemented that 3–1-1 policy. Between Terri and me, we were carrying everything but the kitchen sink in our carry-on and backpacks!

Ino and Gloria Bocobo picked us up for some rest and relaxation between flights at Honolulu. It was, once again, a bittersweet time for me. I was leaving friends who had been like family to me, yet the excitement of settling in our own new home was the next step for us!

CHAPTER 21

When I arrived in South Dakota, I was full of hopes and dreams. The Marriott Residence Inn became my home until August 16. While there, I began to conduct the final preparations to close on the house.

On July 28, I also picked up our new Ford Escape and finished all the paperwork. Then I drove off to see the new house.

Much to my surprise, the decks weren't yet on the house. I guess I was thinking that the builder wouldn't wait until the last minute to complete our home. I picked out the exterior paint and wouldn't see that on the house until forty-eight hours before I moved in! I had to laugh thinking that most South Dakotans aren't really the "hang loose" type of people, so I couldn't figure out why we were now rushing to complete our home.

As far as the house building going on, well, I really found

out firsthand how difficult it was going to be to finish this project without Rich right there. I had forgotten about the ingrained Midwest male mentality towards females. It seemed that I was being simply tolerated by the builder's staff and that they didn't take me seriously at times during the process. I am also supposing that the intensity for me was at a different level and more highly personal than it was for them.

I encountered problem after problem to solve after I began asking questions and expecting cooperation to close our house on time. My main goal was to have everything completely done and in order by the time Rich came in on leave August 28.

Luckily for me, Sioux Falls was very hot and humid that first month. This was just like back home on Kauai for me. I loved it. With all the running around I had to do to pick out furniture for the house, the weather was fully cooperating! The only thing missing was an ocean. It seemed weird not to be able to see the water off in a distance.

My mom, who lived seventy miles away, came into town to stay a couple of days with me. She helped me shop for furniture. We actually purchased all the appliances and furniture for the house on two trips! Then we ordered window coverings for the home. We got a lot accomplished while she stayed with me.

I scheduled all of the deliveries of the furniture, appliances, and shades for the sixteenth and seventeenth of August. It was a huge job, and I was glad for the help and companionship of family and friends during that time.

The week before closing on the house, Charlotte and her friend Steve drove in from Colorado Springs. They were the first people to view the house. I was really pleased with their approval of the house and the site. Steve reported that we had done a good job with the windows and the placing of the home on the lot. Charlotte loved the way the sun came up in the east and poured into the house moving across the south side and in through the windows finally setting in the west outside of our picture window in the living room. She noticed that the foyer window was like a picture frame in the way it looked out over a nature preserve with a huge cottonwood tree right in the middle! I told her that to me, our front foyer window was exactly like a perfectly framed painting! We had a short but quality visit before they went back to Colorado. I was encouraged by our discussions and believed that Rich would love his new home as well.

Again, Marian and Terri were right there and helped me on moving day. It was such a relief to leave the motel and actually pull up to the new home that Rich had purchased for us. Terri arranged for my boxes that had been shipped ahead from Kauai to Marian's home to be picked up, and we worked for three days on unpacking those. We were also able to get Rich's toolbox transported, which was being stored at a friend's home in Sioux Falls. My uncle had been in charge of that for Rich. I knew that Rich would be very excited to come home to a permanent place, one that was his.

I took the moving in and settling into the home, as a labor of love. It was so exciting for me to think ahead and imagine what Rich would think when he first walked in. That is what kept me motivated and moving forward to finish the daunting task.

Our niece, Laurie, came over for a couple of those days

early on and helped me finish unpacking, and we put some order to the house. She brought us a lawn mower and tackled the weeds in the yard. It was a joy and so very peaceful to settle down into our room that first night in the house, August 16, 2008. I couldn't wait for Rich to get in.

Rich was grateful for this niece, who had already been a tremendous help to me. She is there any time I need her. She is also totally supportive of her uncle and his position and work in Iraq. Most of Rich's family has been so proud of him. They have always told him they would be here for me. They have been.

I also began to plan some special outings for Rich's much-anticipated leave. These plans included attending the South Dakota State Fair. We planned to attend a country-western show over Labor Day weekend. I purchased the tickets for Chris, his kids, and my mom to attend with us. It was to be the first time we would all be together for an event in a long time.

Of course, when we have someone deployed or waiting for deployment, we have to expect the unexpected! Chris got the phone call that his training in Houston would begin on August 28. This was the same day that Rich was due home. I couldn't believe it. All of our plans would change regarding Chris, and he would miss seeing his dad here in South Dakota. We didn't have very high hopes of seeing the grandchildren then, either. We wouldn't be able to schedule a Kansas City trip for his homecoming!

So, it was a disappointment for all of us. Chris wouldn't make it up to see his dad. However, he did bring the kids up the very first weekend that I was in the house. It was a

  Linda J. Johnson

wonderful visit, and we were all so excited that they were the first visitors in Grandpa's house.

We had a grand time, and they all loved the house! It was so good to see them. We hadn't seen them since January, and now they knew Grandma and Grandpa were closer to them by reminding me that they only had a six-hour car drive, rather than three airplane rides to get to us!

Chris and I also prepared his power of attorney designating me as his primary attorney in fact. We copied all of his file and papers that he had sent into the company. I kept a duplicate copy of everything that Chris had filled out here.

We all phoned Grandpa, and he got to talk to those happy grandbabies. I had pictures for them to see and take with them of Grandpa, and we all went to church together. Chris was caught in an emotional dilemma. He was happy to see the house, and at the same time, he was sad to be leaving his kids behind in Kansas City.

CHAPTER 22

The flexibility to accept the change of circumstances that came at me so fast was at times non-existent. When I asked Chris to ask if he could change his leave date, he told me that I needed to take a reality check. He had been waiting for the call, and when the company called, he needed to go on their terms. He told me, "Mom, you don't mess with what they request because there are more than enough applicants and men ready to take my spot and go." So, that was that.

When they called, Chris had to get ready to go, period. There have always been plenty of candidates and applicants for these positions, and there still is. Men are waiting their turn to go to Iraq, and most especially with a company like ours. He knew somewhat what to expect, and our company hadn't suffered many casualties in-country. His dad had been sharing with him what would be expected, and Chris would be joining his father and Rich's close friends, so the risk didn't seem as great for him.

In addition, our men, who are actually subcontractors, work "inside the wire," and that gives us some sense of safety and peace. The combat troops work together with our men, but they are responsible for the patrolling "outside the wire." Our men aren't allowed outside the wire or off base, so their positions are considered safer than many. We family members can identify on a map where they are permanently based inside Iraq, and it is a comfort to have that knowledge.

Above all, Chris felt he could probably move up the ranks inside the company due to his financial management background, and this would allow him to earn more money than he had earned in the previous years. Chris also wanted to re-establish himself as the sole provider for his kids and give them a better life. He felt he would become a hero to those little ones, and he achieved that.

Rich, Chris, and I are amazed at how many men are in Iraq from Texas. The recruiters have been busy there at the bases. They know that many men in Texas have a difficult time finding work to support their families. According to many who deploy as contractors, the jobs available inside Texas don't pay enough to feed their families as what they can earn inside Iraq. According to those contractors from Texas, another reason that Texas has such a tough job market is competition for jobs from legal and illegal immigrants, which tends to drive down the wages. This, of course, now includes many other states within the U.S.A.

The lure of the money, benefits, and doing their part is very strong. Rich and Chris would tell me that to them it

  Linda J. Johnson

appeared that two out of five guys were from Texas inside their company. It's hard to document this exactly because contracting companies, along with their subcontractors, give no statistics. We cannot find data on all the employees inside Iraq. That has been a bone of contention to Americans when the media and press have asked the questions but have not been given any answers. They aren't entitled to this information any more than the rest of us. When the media then, in turn, queries us, we don't know what to answer or how to give them any definitive data!

Also, just by the experience that Rich and Chris have had with LSI, it appears to them that six out of the ten employees they work with have had military backgrounds. The recruiters for the Defense Department companies focus their efforts in states that have large army bases and in *Military Times* newspapers, because they believe that those people will have a better chance of adjusting to the demands of contracting work, especially in a war zone. Military background and experience is definitely a positive on a contractor's resume.

Both Rich and Chris have seen a preference for promotions and positions given to veterans within the company. This phenomenon is nationwide. Rich has always told me that many of the men they get in as wheel mechanics lack extensive experience. However, they are hired on. Also, there is a certain degree of cronyism going on within the company. Those in management recruit their friends and family members back in the states for positions to deploy to Iraq. There has been a bonus system in place for referrals that pays the men $1,000 for every man hired. It is paid to the referring employee when the new hire successfully completes six months inside Iraq.

The military is always first in Iraq. In fact, some of the army gives our group a hard time. After all, they are at the front of the bus, so to speak, and our men have to take a backseat. This can be explained by a five-tier ranking of Americans in Iraq. First in line are the active military; then the Department of Defense employees; then the military contractors who are vets; then the military contractors who haven't been vets, and then the private, independent contractors. That pretty much sums up the hierarchy of Iraq and Afghanistan deployments, in my opinion.

It has always puzzled me as to why American newspapers don't report the human death toll in Iraq or Afghanistan by counting the contractor casualties as well. It's as if the price our families pay doesn't matter. The mainstream media appeared only to become aware during the year of 2007 that we are there in large numbers. I was finally able to go to the Web site icasualty.org to find statistics on casualties of civilian contractors inside Iraq. The list keeps growing, but an American contractor who dies in Iraq is usually given just local press coverage in his hometown.

Various newspapers and media are now attempting to inform the public about the role of contractors and the military in Iraq. They have even speculated about the expanding nature of the contractor's growing roles ahead of the recent presidential election in order to mobilize an American electorate backlash towards any good that had been done in Iraq.

After reading the following article, I would have cause to worry about the possibility that my husband or others could

  Linda J. Johnson

be turned over to Iraqi officials on a whim, rather than to our military for responsibility of any illegal actions inside Iraq. This would imply that such a move is necessary due to this possibly being a regular occurrence. Those of us involved in Iraq know that this isn't the case. Contractors or our military transgressing against the Iraqi people has been very limited during the past five years.

If I were a member of the unknowing public in America, I would read the following portions of this article and immediately see the word secret and then speculate as to the cost and necessity of our military or contractors in Iraq. In addition, this type of article would possibly cause me to conclude that the Iraq war has caused the downfall of our economy and we should be out of there. Hence, this conclusion mobilizes anti-war protestors and others against anyone inside Iraq and causes a larger division among Americans than the one that already exists.

> *A secret deal being negotiated in Baghdad would perpetuate the American military occupation of Iraq indefinitely, regardless of the outcome of the US presidential election in November.*
>
> The timing of the agreement would also boost the Republican candidate, John McCain, who has claimed the United States is on the verge of victory in Iraq–a victory that he says Mr. Obama would throw away by a premature military withdrawal.
>
> *America currently has 151,000 troops in Iraq and, even after projected withdrawals next month, troop levels will stand at more than 142,000–10,000 more than when the military "surge" began in January 2007.*

Under the terms of the new treaty, the Americans would retain the long-term use of more than 50 bases in Iraq. American negotiators are also demanding immunity from Iraqi law for US troops and contractors, and a free hand to carry out arrests and conduct military activities in Iraq without consulting the Baghdad government.

The precise nature of the American demands has been kept secret until now. The leaks are certain to generate an angry backlash in Iraq. "It is a terrible breach of our sovereignty," said one Iraqi politician, adding that if the security deal was signed it would delegitimise the government in Baghdad which will be seen as an American pawn. [1]

I believe that the press has been somewhat irresponsible in covering the Iraq war and biased in their reporting, and I am suspicious about the media's motives. Our men appear to be used for the media's political agenda of telling the American taxpayer that contractors' jobs are costly and possibly unnecessary and that we need to end the Iraq war and leave dishonorably. At least, that is what I am reading into these articles and conversations with those who oppose Iraq and blame President Bush for the economic downturn of America at present.

I may even speculate that the media has caused a lot of the lack of goodwill among other nations towards America due to their one-sided coverage and indictment on President Bush regarding the Iraq war. They might look in the mirror as they remind all Americans how "unpopular" we are!

While many Americans will say that they support our troops, they will stand up openly and even march against whatever has been accomplished to stabilize Iraq and the Middle East. I don't see how anyone can divorce their true feelings and objections to the conflicts in the Middle East by saying they are supportive of our efforts. Certainly, if the American public is made to believe day after day that military contractors shouldn't be there or that there is no need, or that they were "duped" by President Bush, then a job or the role someone like my husband has played is in vain. I don't and won't ever believe that.

CHAPTER 23

Despite all of this, Chris left for Houston from Kansas City the day before his dad arrived in Sioux Falls. I was excited for Rich to see his new home yet full of anxiety and worry for Chris. I was also sad for his children, who were left behind in Kansas City.

I found out that this time I couldn't isolate myself a few days prior to his coming in, as I had done in the past, or for a few days after he left. Usually I will be sure to adjust myself to the coming and going without taking it out on anyone else. These days after he leaves, I spend time reflecting on our last leave. Then I pray that I will make the right decisions this next segment of time, until he comes home again. It's very hard. There had been too much to do and I had had Chris' family there up until a few days before Rich arrived. I was sure that when he left again, I would hit "rock bottom"

and take a break from all of the changes that had occurred and get myself ready to support two of them deployed!

With this being Rich's third leave, we already knew the drill. The airlines allowed me a pass to the gate to meet him. They have mostly always been very cooperative and supportive to us. After all, Rich is under military orders and attached to the army. Some people and companies have respected that and have helped me out a lot due to that. Once I explain our role in this conflict, many will thank Rich or me for giving a spouse and a son to the effort. They are amazed at my ability to cope alone during this journey.

The first minute that Rich viewed our house, he fell in love with it. Thank goodness he approved of all that I had decided upon. He even loved the outside paint color that I had had to choose separately from what he and I originally agreed upon. It turned out that the paint color we had thought would work didn't present itself upon the model home like I thought it would. I took a chance then and asked the paint store manager in Sioux Falls to help me decide upon a neutral color in between the colors available for us to choose from on the builder's existing model homes. I didn't think Rich would choose the lightest or the next lighter shade choices that we had. The builder only gave me twenty-four hours to choose a different shade at the paint store, and I had to sign a waiver to not hold them responsible after it was applied to the house! Once again, it all worked out with the "Nantucket dunes" color. I hadn't been sure if he would approve of that because I couldn't e-mail him a picture of this color anywhere on an existing home. However, he told me it was exactly what he would've chosen. He also loved the furniture and appliances chosen, and he was very pleased.

My mother later commented that she couldn't believe that the rug Rich had sent in from Iraq to be placed under our new dining room table exactly matched the blinds and décor of the house and he hadn't even seen the house yet! She said, "Yup, you two have been married twenty-nine years all right to be able to pick out exact same shades, even down to a rug for under the kitchen table while you are miles apart."

We held a house blessing on Labor Day weekend. My mom and Rich's family, along with some friends, attended our catered event. It was a very special time for us. I made a commitment to Rich that I would have his back here in South Dakota while he worked in those conditions for our future.

Rich brought home his awards and medals received to date when he came in. These included gold coins and medals awarded to him by the company and the military. We proudly displayed them for all to see. He also brought back an awesome CD given to him by the staff sergeant of the A company, 425th Civil Affairs Battalion. She had awarded to our men numerous medals and certificates. She had also taken some awesome pictures over the period of almost two years that her unit was deployed.

These pictures included the "shock and awe" campaign, as well as mosques, churches, cities, and the people of Iraq. The pictures had been shot all over Iraq. She had been the army's liaison officer for visiting U.S. dignitaries for quite a long time. One day we will share those with everyone.

Rich also brought home the monthly safety award and a coin given to him from the company. Only a small percentage of men receive this award. It is a coveted award throughout the company. I could see he was in his element and very appreciated for what he was doing there. I was so proud of him! This is the wording of that award:

> Richard sets an example that every employee hopes to see. He is first on the floor each morning, and the last to leave. If our work load slows down, he takes the initiative to clean, make repairs, and fix the shop, or work area. He is safety orientated, keeping us on our toes by identifying potential safety hazards.
>
> He puts the customer and team members' needs before his own. He exhibits a strong work ethic, and is knowledgeable in his area of expertise. He produces high qualify workmanship. Staying safe is a factor in all he does.
>
> Mr. Johnson is enthusiastic, trustworthy, and maintains endurance, integrity, bearing, justice, good judgment and is decisive, and always punctual. Richard can be left unsupervised and trusted to make the right decisions. He is well respected by the Military that we serve, other LSI employees, and myself. Richard Johnson is an excellent representative for LSI.

He also had awards given to him by the 21st Light Infantry Battalion and the 4th Brigade 31D of the Georgian Army. Rich had been a foreman and supervisor over at Grey Wolf /FOB with the Georgian Army for the first five months inside Baghdad.

Rich had also been awarded a certificate from the 3rd Brigade Special Police Transition team, who helped to initially train the Iraqis.

  Linda J. Johnson

He was getting *vast* experience and exposure to the other multinational forces in Iraq during his first year there, and the company had extended his contract for a second year. Rich and I had decided right before his leave that he would sign on for year two.

It appeared that this would be the only way we could pay cash for the yard we needed to complete, and pay off our bills for the furniture.

He also wanted to finish the second level of the house, and we would need that extra income that he would not be able to earn in South Dakota. His buddies inside Iraq also told Rich that by staying on and gaining the experience on a military base he was giving himself a better chance for future employment in the States. Rich definitely didn't want to leave with Chris just going into Iraq either, so the decision was made. I felt a certain peace about this because I was now living close to family and in our home state. Besides, they would both be together and I felt Rich could help Chris adjust and excel.

We decided to schedule our next leave in early 2007 for somewhere other than the U.S.A. This would help to satisfy the number of months he needed out-of-country for the tax-free exemption status that he now qualified for. By making this decision, we both knew he wouldn't be back in his home for nine long months. We chose Athens, Greece, for the next leave. He wouldn't have to travel as far, and I could use his accumulated airline points to get a ticket over there. Greece as a destination place had been suggested to Rich earlier by his administrator on base, so we e-mailed the administrator and put in the request.

We have been fortunate while Rich was deployed for the first three years to have an excellent administrator on-site. He was a former navy guy who had been at D-2 since before Rich got there. James (name changed) kept me informed and acted as a go-between when I had questions for Rich. He was very good at what he did. That gave me a sense of connection to Rich also, in a more personal way. I could always reach James by e-mail if I couldn't get to Rich. He responded almost instantly, and then I knew what was happening.

James also sent me changes to policy and other reminders for administrative purposes relating to Rich. He has been there to fend for the men since day one and was in full support of all the families affected in the unit. Rich was rooming with James for a few months also when the housing units became full. As the site filled up, most of the men at D-2 had to share quarters from the summer of 2008 on. They were told that no new housing units would be brought in.

We made the most of his twenty-one days that first summer he was home. It seems we packed so much into his time home that the days flew by. He secured his South Dakota driver's license, and we now had a permanent place to hang our hats! I was so proud of Rich because it was his hard-earned money that purchased our home. He did it all by himself!

We also made a big decision to plant four matured trees in our yard rather than do the landscaping or put in the sod. We decided we could wait for the spring/summer of 2007 for the lawn.

One reason we decided to do this also was that we now had a privacy issue to the north of our newly-built home. The builder had built a house there and put that neighbor's

  Linda J. Johnson

patio/deck facing our bedroom window. We had looked at the plans on that corner lot and decided not to make an offer on it when it was available originally. Instead, we purchased our specific lot.

We really made a big assumption when we thought that the builder would swing any house on that lot to an angle. If he would have, like pictures on their Web site had shown, then there wouldn't have been as much of a problem with noise from the neighbors when they were on their deck drifting into our bedroom. Later, we asked our neighbors about it, and sure enough, they thought their home was scheduled to be angled on that lot too. They told us that they were shocked to come and find the driveway poured straight west. So, this was another expense for us that we hadn't planned for.

We had not yet realized how many problems we were going to have in the days to come with our builder. Problem after problem arose, and it almost seemed to us that he created some of them to affect us personally. I was faced with dealing with all the stress of the problems alone once again. It was awful. Apparently this is one reason why so many people have told me that they don't build a new house. It's easier to just purchase an existing one! I'm not yet sure what we think, because our problems aren't over.

CHAPTER 24

During that August, Rich was interviewed by our local newspaper, the *Argus Leader*. He and I were both concerned about the growing misperception as well as ignorance that people displayed regarding the role of our men in Iraq. We were getting more questions from family and friends when Rich signed on for that second year. When we informed people of Chris's deployment, in addition to Rich's, people wanted to know how many and just who were deployed as military contractors, and what did they all do?

The mainstream media and press, along with talk show hosts and major news channels, were now openly bashing President Bush and the Iraq war on a regular basis. It felt personal to me, and it seemed that anyone who was involved in Iraq was now the "enemy." We wanted to attempt to get the word out in a more personal way and show people that many Americans, like my husband, inside Iraq were helping to cross the cultural barrier and actually contributing to the local economy while being there.

We contacted the *Argus* and told them about the Iraqi vases that he had brought home to display in our front windows. They were very interested in speaking with him about the story surrounding his securing of that art. They wanted to highlight the story of what he had to go through to get them home.

A reporter came over with a photographer on the afternoon of September 7. They spent over two hours talking to Rich about Iraq. He explained a lot of what he does, and we showed them his medals and awards. Then he discussed the story behind getting the vases for me. For us it was a great opportunity to educate the public and put a face on a military contractor. They took a lot of pictures and told us they would let us know when the story would run.

The story ran on September 18. This was one day after Rich had gone back to Iraq. We were on the front page, and the online story featured him. It was a great article, and we heard lots of favorable comments about it.

Rich was able to get a copy of the story to the Iraqi men who had found the vases for him. They proudly displayed it on the wall. They have it up to this day in their little shop inside the Green Zone! The title of the story was "Man searches for gift in Iraq, finds friends." Here are some of the highlights of what was said.

A man's search for a gift for his wife in a war-torn country has led him to unique art and a transatlantic friendship.
Richard Johnson, 52, is working as a mechanic

  Linda J. Johnson

for a military contractor in Iraq. His wife wanted a memento of his work abroad, and asked him to bring back vases for the entryway of their house.

Little did the couple know her request would lead them to forge a bond with Iraqi men who, the Johnsons said, willingly took a risk to get three silver vases for the couple's modest home.

"It's for a memory, a keepsake," Linda said. "It's the Mid East coming to the Midwest."

She asked a Lebanese friend for advice in choosing art unique to Iraq, and was told silver vases would be a good choice because they are rare compared to gold vases in the country.

Meanwhile, the three Iraqi men went in search of silver vases. They each lived outside the Green Zone. One of them had to take several different cabs through dangerous parts of the city, so people would not know what he was doing.

Richard said there is some suspicion among Iraqis and that not all are willing to do business with Americans. Therefore, the three men were discrete as they looked for the vases.

During the five-week search, Richard and the men formed a bond. They asked him about his family, South Dakota, and Christmas.

"This became personal," Linda said. "Now they want pictures, and they want to know (about us)."[1]

Rich is usually very careful about giving out any family information to local residents of Iraq; however, this venture proved to be a bonding between him and the shop owners. Rich still sees the newspaper picture hanging up in the shop to this day, and these men consider themselves now friends of my husband. They are always happy to see him, and whenever he needs even a postcard or small item, he checks at their shop first to give them his business!

Even though there have been some very good cross-cultural experiences with the Iraqi people living and working inside the Green Zone, our men still shred all mail and any return addresses coming in on boxes or letters so as not to identify us personally. This is for safety reasons.

This became a much more important task at the end of 2006, when we were all told that if the enemy of America's mission in Iraq couldn't get to our men, they would get to the loved ones waiting back home, within the U.S.A. That was sobering news for all of us.

  Linda J. Johnson

CHAPTER 25

In the meantime, Rich was reunited with Chris at D-2 inside Iraq, and they were both very happy to be together. I reminded them both that it is rare for a father and son to get an opportunity to spend this kind of time together in their adult lives. I told them to make the most of it. Now I had two loved ones in there to worry about.

We know now, in fact, that there are many fathers and sons working together in Iraq or stationed on the same bases. It has happened more than we realize during this conflict.

I began to make plans for our February 2007 leave to Athens, Greece, right after he left. I reached the Filipino family we had lived with on Kauai, and Shirley promised to extend her friends and family discount to us for the Marriott hotel there. So, I made that reservation. My ticket, using Rich's accumulated American Airline points, only cost us $106. For the first leg of that flight, from Sioux Falls to Minneapolis, I used points on my Northwest account and paid $10 for that ticket. All in all, the upcoming leave wasn't going to be too expensive for us, and it would be a great way to kick off our thirtieth wedding anniversary year. We both began to look forward to the getaway time we would have together in Greece.

The holiday season of 2006 loomed in front of me, and I would spend it without Rich again. This year I would have a chance to spend it with some of my family. Rich would be inside Iraq with Chris, and that relieved me somehow. And our niece Laurie had committed to helping out with the Christmas project for the men at D-2.

She had a girlfriend, who was her neighbor, who was leading a Girl Scout troop, and those girls planned to sponsor our men as their service project for the year. I was so thankful knowing that we were going to be able to help them have a Merry Christmas while they were all so far from home.

That October, I also traveled to Bismarck, North Dakota, for our regional ministers' meetings. A girlfriend rode up with me to help drive. We planned an additional visit to a well-known cathedral in a small South Dakota town on our way back.

During this trip, however, Rich and Chris were sent again to the bunkers. After a day of meetings in Bismarck, I was working out on a treadmill in the hotel and watching Fox News. A report came on that Baghdad was burning due to one of our ammunition dumps getting burned. The reporter mentioned that the incident occurred inside the Green Zone or in close proximity. I was shocked and I panicked. We had so many reports going on so often of bombings, security

  Linda J. Johnson

breeches, and untoward activity during that timeframe. It was very unnerving.

I immediately tried Rich's phone and couldn't reach him. There was no signal, and/or he had his phone off. I kept trying, frantic to know what was really happening.

When I finally reached him later that night, around 10:00 p.m. (early morning his time), he promised to call me back after morning report.

At midnight we finally talked. He said an incident had occurred at a munitions stockpile at a FOB nearby to them. The soldiers there and company personnel got out with only the shirts on their backs. Everything burned. Rich couldn't tell me the specific details, and of course, the media didn't know exactly what was happening, and they wouldn't ever know the entire story due to the fact that those incidents were classified and the reports that had to be made were only for the military and the company involved, not the press.

For five of our own employees, everything they owned was gone, including their own personal bunks. The company personnel located at D-2 were scrambling to collect personal items and clothing for these men. They also took a money collection.

I was sick to my stomach. I knew what most people didn't know—these guys were left with nothing. Even if we quickly packed boxes for all of them, they still wouldn't receive them for over a week to ten days.

It touched my heart when Rich told me that each man in his unit was giving up socks, jeans, shirts, and even hygiene items, along with money, to try and help these guys out. Chris was scrambling to pick out "new" items from his personal belongings so he could help out those guys.

This effort became company-wide from base to base. Within twenty-four hours, the men affected were benefiting from the care and generosity of their brothers and sisters. Of course, the army took care of their soldiers with army issue. It was much less of a problem for them.

On November 13, I got another strange call from Rich, and it took me a while to get him to explain just exactly what was up. He just didn't sound like himself. Apparently, according to Chris, this is what happened.

The men were at the work site when another loud explosion occurred. Not one hundred feet from Rich and Chris's bay, body parts landed. Apparently a terrorist had strapped himself with explosives and rushed the wall. He had been covered in so many explosives that his body broke apart and flew a thousand yards or more over the walls. The men were stunned! Outside the walls, a vehicle exploded at the same time, killing innocent Iraqi civilians.

This incident affected Rich adversely more than at any other time that he was inside Iraq. From that point on, he changed. I also knew the impact was greater upon him for this incident because Chris was there with him. I think Rich moved into a father or protective role, and he definitely didn't like what had happened.

I couldn't get over the fact that someone's son, brother, father, or husband had blown himself to pieces for the sake of making a strike for Islam. We understand the overall mission of the extremists within the Islamic religion and their hatred for the West, but this action was pointless to us. It was unreal to me. For Rich and Chris and the men at D-2, it brought it all home and up close, front, and personal.

  Linda J. Johnson

As a CISD (critical incident stress debriefing) chaplain, I wished I could have been there that day to talk with all the people affected. Chris told me, "Mom, you are never coming here. Your job is to stay at home, support us, and back us up. We know you are safe there and always ready to take our calls or e-mails. That is where we need you." So, that was the end of my thinking I would go to Iraq! However, I have had many days since when I wished that I could go over there to do my part.

The first weekend of December, I met with the Girl Scouts troop who were going to sponsor our men for Christmas. I had prepared a presentation for the girls and had written a letter of thanks and explanation for them to take home to their families. After speaking to them about our role there and showing pictures of Rich and Chris and some of the men, we all went to work.

The girls had brought everything including coffee, beef jerky, and Christmas candies for packing. They also wrote personal letters and made Christmas crafts for each man. Then we looked through the items that the girls brought to send.

It would be such an encouragement for those men to receive the letters, boxes, and personal items made just for them. It was such a critical time for us in Iraq, and these boxes were going to some tired and worn out men. I was so excited knowing the blessing this project would be to all of them deployed there at D-2.

Our government was still holding Saddam Hussein, and the world had been watching his trial on TV. It was like a circus at times. Rich said that the politics between the different Iraqi groups drove the fighting. This fact, along with a hate mission by those insurgents who wanted Americans dead, caused lots of problems within Iraq and Baghdad as a whole.

At the same time, the news began to report that Saddam would be executed. Rich said they were put on alert over there and that they expected some trouble when the actual execution was set. He said it would happen after Christmas but before New Year's.

PHOTOS

One of Linda's favorite pictures of Rich in Honolulu the day he left for Houston and processing for Iraq. August 5, 2005.

These statues of Saddam Hussein were stored nearby to Rich's work site for a few months after they were removed from public places.

Rich at the Hands of Victory, a triumphal arch built by Saddam to commemorate Iraq's victory over Iran. October 2005 in Baghdad.

Rich's first Christmas in Iraq. Christmas day at the DFAC/Camp Prosperity. 2005.

Linda J. Johnson

The hooches look almost like a stateside mobile home park!

The housing units for Rich and his team at D-2.

*Rich with an Iraqi security/police offi-
cer inside the Green Zone. April 2006.*

*Rich on tour of monuments inside
Green Zone. Spring of 2006.*

  Linda J. Johnson

A picture of Grandpa for the grandkids back home.

A vehicle waiting for the customer to pick up!

Rich in his own bay at D-2.

An incoming helicopter nearby to the chapel that Rich attended regularly on Sunday evenings.

  Linda J. Johnson

*The view looks almost normal here on the route
to the chapel inside Baghdad's Green Zone.*

Rich receiving an Army award in Summer of 2006.

Chris and Rich inside Iraq early 2007 at D-2.

A strange sight over Baghdad at sun-
set ... after an explosion on the ground.

Linda J. Johnson

Level Black inside D-2. Rich with his best buddy, Terry.

Rich with his buddy Terry on the job site at D-2, Baghdad.

*Scenes from inside and outside of the blast walls
in March of 2007 following another explosion.*

  Linda J. Johnson

Rich is running toward a "hard cover" building at the end of April 2007 while bridges were being targeted outside the walls.

The surprise thirtieth wedding anniver-
sary gift to Rich, with most of his awards to-date
showcased for his first two years inside Iraq.

The largest case includes his Award of Excellence
from the company, as well as the Presidential Award
for support. Chris is featured with his dad also.

  Linda J. Johnson

A sandstorm approaching Al Asad Air Base in Iraq, 2007.

A certificate of appreciation for two full years of service at the end of August 2007, which reads in part, "THIS EFFORT HAS MADE A DIFFERENCE IN THE LIVES OF THE SOLDIERS, SAILORS, AIRMEN & MARINES ... GENERATIONS TO COME WILL BENEFIT FROM YOUR STALWART EFFORTS ..."

Rich and Linda Johnson. Thirtieth wedding anniversary, November 2007.

Richard Johnson inside Baghdad's Green Zone. July 2, 2008.

  Linda J. Johnson

CHAPTER 26

I was going to be going back to Colorado for the week between Christmas and New Year's. I had just been there for a week in October to see a very dear friend and my sisters living there. We had plans to hold a family baptism for one of my great-nieces, and I would officiate.

The Christmas holidays sprang upon us with cold and snow predicted. I packed the car to go to Rich's family for Christmas Eve and then on to my mom's home for a later church service. I felt that emptiness inside again, knowing I would be solo at these family events. After a while, I have gotten used to it, even though he had missed so many family gatherings. Neither one of us could've foreseen that these holiday times would be spent apart from each other on a regular basis.

The day after Christmas, my mother and I were heading out from Mitchell, South Dakota, to Colorado, and we were going to drive halfway to Boulder. A blizzard warning was issued. We were headed right into it. What was supposed to be a week away from home extended to almost two weeks for me!

I had forgotten the nuisance of winter driving. Another obstacle for me to overcome was my confidence in my own ability to drive in winter weather without Rich. That Christmas, I had no choice! We were snowed in at Colorado, and I didn't get home until January 4.

During the family gathering at Boulder, sure enough, as I was talking to Rich from Baghdad, the TV was reporting that Saddam had been executed. Rich confirmed this and said the base was on alert anticipating more activity from supporters of Saddam and his former Baathist party. The direct retribution never came the way our media was reporting. Rich told me that later on. He said a sense of relief washed over many Iraqis and the Americans stationed there when nothing happened.

Also while I was in Colorado that holiday season, it dawned on me that this being alone when one is married is a strange way to live! Rich and I joked that as busy as I appeared to be, the only social life I could have with him away was events with family and close friends or church events! Nothing else was appropriate or desirous without him. Even that holiday season, I didn't realize I would still be waiting into the year 2009 and that we wouldn't yet make a decision for him to come home.

We both laugh when I remind him that I have gone to a new movie alone, and he writes it down if it is something that I tell him he would enjoy watching on DVD. He can get many of the latest release movies at the PX and even some

Linda J. Johnson

copies of brand new movies that are still in theaters! He tells me they are poor copies, however, and it isn't the same as if we were together!

We have learned to take one day at a time on this journey, and a new year was beginning for both of us. Chris was due back at home in Kansas City for a leave in January, and I would get to see him and his kids.

At the same time, my very good friend and encourager, Ron Jarman, had continued to battle his colon cancer. He was failing, but I didn't realize that he was in the end stages of his life.

We planned that I would go down to Kansas City to see Chris and finally get to visit Ron. However, on January 9, 2007, I got the terrible phone call from Ron's son—Ron had passed away peacefully in his apartment that day. I was so stunned and so very sad. I had been preoccupied with trying to get home after the holidays and didn't talk to him daily as usual. Now I wouldn't be able to talk to him again. I phoned Rich, and we both prayed for guidance in the days ahead.

Instead of going down to see a friend who had been an invaluable source of encouragement for Rich, Chris, and I, I was going down to his funeral. The family had asked that I attend, if I could, and speak a few words to those gathered at the small military funeral.

It was so sad, really sad. I didn't realize how much Ron's death would affect me. He was a voice that was always there when I needed to talk about anything. Having been in the air force and retired, he completely understood the role of military contractors and mentioned frequently that he had worked with many of them in WWII while stationed in Germany. He cut interesting articles out of the newspaper to send in to

Rich and Chris from Kansas City, and he knew how to help in small ways to keep them connected to home. He was the strongest male advocate for Rich and Chris that we had here in the States, other than other contractors. He was a wealth of information for us also in that he would relay breaking news coming into Kansas City and clip articles relevant to the war.

He always encouraged, listened, and advised. Now he was gone. It was sad and tragic. The colon cancer took his life within six months of diagnosis. My only consolation was that both Rich and I remembered him as he was in the summer of 2005, healthy and jovial. Maybe that's the way he wanted it. We would never have to see him when he was down. It wasn't meant to be. It was still a hard reality for me to accept. It couldn't be possible that he was gone.

I attended his funeral with Floyd Thomas, one of the former elders of our pastorate from Kansas City. Floyd had helped Ron through the last few months of his life. It was harder on Floyd, I think, than anyone else. Ron had given Floyd some additional purpose to his life. Floyd took his role as a caretaker very seriously during that last six months of Ron's life. He even drove Ron to many of his doctor's appointments. We both participated in the funeral at Topeka, Kansas. At the small family gathering, his son, his brother, and extended family were very grateful that we had attended.

Ron was given full military rights from the air force he had retired from. It was a cold and sad day when we bid our old friend good-bye. Rich really got it when I told him I was reluctant to take Ron's phone number out of my phone. It would seem like then that he was really gone. All Rich could

  Linda J. Johnson

say was, "Well, you are home now with friends and family, and Ron is at his final home."

As Rich and I looked forward to 2007, we realized that we had come through so many trials and tribulations already. We would be celebrating thirty years of marriage that year. Rich would face a decision whether to stay the course or come home and look for work.

He decided to stay on because he wanted to complete the second level of our home. He felt this was the only opportunity we would have to get this done, and better then than never. I knew that this meant that he would be deployed possibly two more years or longer!

CHAPTER 27

The downstairs would be a big project, and we were only just paying off the upstairs furniture. We would also have the lawn to put in and the landscaping to be done. It was always something else with a new house, and we didn't want to borrow for those things.

We also knew that things would probably settle down inside Baghdad because the surge was about to happen. The media was predicting it, but they were clueless, as usual, as to just what this meant for our country and OIF (Operation Iraqi Freedom). They wouldn't admit or realize until much later that the surge was one of the most successful strategies for securing peace inside Baghdad. The surge also brought a steady decline in Americans' deaths inside Iraq and brought a sense of order to the country. Rich and Chris thought all along that more troops present in Baghdad would calm down the daily chaos and discourage the insurgents' activity. It did!

I had a plane reservation for February 2, 2007, to Athens, Greece, via Minneapolis, Chicago, and London. Rich would start to be moved a few days before his leave to catch a flight from Dubai to meet me in Athens. He was scheduled to leave Dubai on February 2, in the morning. That meant he would have to leave BTC (Baghdad airport) sometime on February 1.

There was only one problem—Rich's flight out to Dubai might've gotten cancelled! The motor pool sergeant with the army inside Baghdad told Rich that there was a possibility the Baghdad airport would close down due to the upcoming surge. This was told to Rich in the strictest of confidence. Rich called me and asked what he should do. If he was transported to Liberty Base (Baghdad airport—BTC) and it closed down, he would be stuck there in Baghdad. He didn't want to take the chance of getting stuck and delayed and possibly not get out of Iraq due to the surge. This would leave me alone in Athens! It was a big dilemma for us.

We both agonized over what to do. First of all, Rich was only cleared for a ten-day leave. Secondly, he couldn't betray the confidence of the motor pool sergeant, who was a good friend. Third, once I began to travel, we would be out of communication, and I could possibly end up on our R and R by myself in Greece! We both knew that this wouldn't work for me.

I was already skittish about leaving the U.S.A. It would be the first time in almost nine years that I would be leaving the U.S.A. for foreign travel. Rich knew that I would be in for a shock with all the changes affecting international travel. He also knew it would exhaust me and be hard on my physical body.

  Linda J. Johnson

The last thing we had to consider was that Rich was leaving Chris behind. He was uncertain as to just what was going to happen during the surge. He had been told they were going into lockdown during the initial sweep of Baghdad. He realized that this would be a dangerous time. The motor pool sergeant told Rich to prepare to stay indoors during the initial sweep/surge because anyone out of place or not part of the military could be shot! So, Rich was worried for Chris. There would also be a blackout for communications, and we wouldn't be able to reach Chris. This would be stressful for both of us, not knowing what was going on during that time.

We both prayed and talked to Chris, and he told his dad to, "Go ahead. If something happens, I would rather have one of us out of here."

Chris and James (name changed) proceeded to secure for Rich an extra day of LWOP (leave without pay) processed for Rich. He would leave the site a day earlier and fly out of Baghdad on January 31, just in case.

Again, Rich couldn't even tell the company site manager or anyone else what was going on because he would be breaking confidentiality. Rich knew that the rest of his company did not have this news. They seemed oblivious as to what was going down.

We have frequently talked about how the American media has no idea what is really going on in Iraq. Foreign media are confined to a certain area within Iraq. The insurgents always put on a show for them there. This is what Rich always tells me. But, he explains, "This isn't the real Iraq."

In the meantime, I was getting ready to leave for Athens,

and I had to register Rich and me with the U.S. Embassy there. The reason for this was because the U.S. Embassy was bombed that January, and they had been sending us travel alerts. We knew we would have to take some precautions during our stay there now. This would be just because we were Americans and due to where Rich was working. They told us to be very wise and cautious as to our activity while in Athens. We were advised to limit our exposure in public places.

Great! This was supposed to be a relaxing getaway for both of us. Now we were both jumpy going in. It appeared that our idyllic vacation plans became a little more challenging than we had hoped for.

Rich, meanwhile, was having a horrible time after he got out of Iraq. In Dubai, he had to pay for his first night's stay at the hotel because he was on an extra day of leave. We knew that and paid for this by credit card. The second day, on February 1, he checked in with the company desk and was given his airline ticket but no key. They told him he wasn't entitled to a room paid for by them because he had arrived a day early in Dubai and was on his own. So, Rich went out to the Dubai airport and slept in a lounge chair waiting for the next day and his flight out to Athens. Yet, he had never gotten his room that he was entitled to from the company in the first place. He had paid for the first night himself. This plan was supposedly worked out by our administration to accommodate Rich's change of schedule, but it wasn't.

When he went to check in for his flight at Dubai airport, he had the wrong airline ticket with him. They had issued and given him his ticket for his next leave, home to South Dakota! His upcoming summer 2007 leave ticket had already been charged to our credit card, and they had printed and given him the future ticket. It had been paid for by us because we were reserving a fourteen-day leave, which would include the Fourth of July in South Dakota. Luckily, Rich had the confirmation number for his correct flight to Athens, and it got straightened out.

By the time he met my plane on Friday evening, February 2, 2007, he was exhausted. He had been up with no sleep since Thursday morning. He was stressed out, worried about Chris, and angry at the company.

It was rainy when my plane landed in Athens. After clearing customs, I passed through those doors, and there he was. He was standing there with a bouquet of flowers and just beaming. We grabbed the first cab and traveled through the streets of Athens. After a long day, we got checked into our hotel and got to the room.

We slept until late Saturday afternoon. I know we didn't venture out of that hotel until Sunday afternoon! I told Rich how kind the U.S. Armed Forces lounge had been to me in Chicago. They let me rest there and sleep between my flights from South Dakota while I waited for a connection to London. All I needed were the copies of Rich's orders, and it was good enough for them. They helped make my long, hard trip bearable.

We spent lots of time just orienting ourselves and getting over jet lag. We had computer and phone access at the Marriott. So, we were able to communicate with the base. Both Charles and Chris were shocked at how the company had treated Rich in Dubai. As usual, the site manager at D-2 wouldn't go to bat for Rich. He stayed out of it. He liked to play it safe and make no waves. I was outraged. Rich had been a reliable employee and never missed a day of work. He deserved to be treated better than that. Rich told me not to worry about it and that he would file a complaint when he got back into Iraq.

In the meantime, we were grateful to hear from Chris that as the surge began, things remained orderly and not chaotic. Thank goodness was all we could say or think. Our men were safe during this time. Also, Chris was busy applying for other positions and a promotion within the company. He had been trained now in administration and wanted a position like that. It could mean more money, and he would be doing the kind of work he loved.

Rich and I went on to have a mostly wonderful, relaxing, and refreshing ten days in Greece. It was nice to be away from everything, including phones, mail, work, and other problems or responsibilities. We signed up for two tours with approved tour groups. One was a city tour of Athens and the surrounding sites, and the other was to Delphi in northern Greece. We both thought this would give us more than enough of the flavor of Greece.

The first time we caught a taxicab to check a famous shopping district near downtown Athens, I noticed the changes in Rich. He was jumpy and nervous. When I entered a shop, he would stand watch and keep his eyes on the street, the door, and the shopkeeper—all at one time! He was clearly spooked by all the traffic and didn't want to be in the crowds. He wouldn't let me hail a cab. He wanted to check out each one himself. I gave up the shopping trip that first Sunday afternoon. After we found him a new leather belt in a shop, I realized we needed to go back to the hotel and talk this out.

Up until that time, Rich had lived in the constant noise of war in Baghdad. Every day for him was all about helicopters taking off and landing, guns, sirens and bombings. It had been a constant for him since he was deployed in August of 2005. This was now February of 2007, and he was overloaded due to his exposure in a combat zone. Maybe he was suffering combat zone fatigue! I wasn't sure, and neither was he. We both realized later on, though, that we probably picked a precarious place to meet. Greece was still pretty close to Iraq, and for Rich, the people looked similar.

The city was crowded with people and vehicles with honking horns, and it was very chaotic. The people themselves, in mannerisms and dress, somewhat resembled those he saw daily. I think he felt like he was outside the wire. Therefore, everything and everyone represented a potential threat to him. In his eyes, just about anyone of any age could be a potential terrorist with a bomb.

Once I realized this, we simplified our stay. I just let him call the shots on where or how far we could go from the hotel. He certainly slept and rested after that. We both did. This trip of a lifetime for us could've happened anywhere in the world. As long as we were together, it didn't matter where we were!

CHAPTER 28

Another interesting thing I noticed while in Greece was that when reading the local newspapers it appeared that Europe and the European Union took the hardliner approach to the Iraq War. It was clearly the general consensus there that the U.S. was wrong to be in Iraq. In fact, anti-U.S.A. sentiment was very strong in Greece. I was shocked and saddened. The hotel kept us informed of demonstrations that went on during two separate days while we were in Athens. These were anti-U.S. demonstrations, and we were advised to steer clear of the downtown plaza area when they were going on.

We got a chance to have a lively and interesting discussion with two Canadian citizens. One was German born, and the other was born in India. They were with us on the tour to Delphi. One was a global speculator and businessman from Toronto, and the other was a doctor from Montréal. When

I explained our family's position as to why we had to stay the course in Iraq, they were impressed. They had already figured out that Rich was inside Iraq.

They both explained that it was difficult to gauge just exactly what Americans really thought. To them, our media had done such a disservice to the American people by portraying us as a divided nation who was not supportive of our military or our president. For them, this was unacceptable. Furthermore, they wondered why more Americans like us weren't speaking out more often.

Of course, I reminded them that we wouldn't get much opportunity to voice out because our media slants politically towards Democrats, those who oppose the war, and those who engage in anti-Iraq rhetoric.

These two gracious men ended our conversation by thanking me for giving up my husband and my son for the cause of America's freedom and security. They also thanked us because they fully believed that without Americans' efforts, the objectives of Islamic extremism would continue on unchecked, resulting in more violence coming to North America.

It was a fruitful day not only for all the magnificent sights we saw, but for the opportunity we had to tell our side of the story. Rich hadn't shared much himself, but he would smile as I made my points throughout the stimulating conversation.

It occurred to me that for those of us who support this effort and understand the ramifications of a withdrawal from Iraq, we are often silently suffering. We don't often vocalize where we stand or how we feel. Yet, we had to endure the onslaught of criticism of our loved ones, our military, and President Bush. It wasn't right.

  Linda J. Johnson

I'm sure that many military families and contractor families have similar mood swings whenever the news comes on and someone bashes our efforts in Iraq. We take this personally. It is like a dripping faucet dripping away at our emotional and mental health. It's hard enough to endure it as it is. But then we have to be demonized. I might add that contractors suffer this attitude against them in greater numbers than the active military. It's tough. With the last presidential election and candidates who clearly stood on an anti-Iraq platform, it has been emotionally exhausting. Sometimes I am actually afraid to turn on the TV or read an article about Iraq. I am never sure what I'm going to read.

Overall, we had such a marvelous ten days in Athens. We had more than enough time to catch up on all that was going on with the house problems and family issues without interruption. Later I thought about what a long way we had to go for this getaway!

The day that we had to say good-bye at the Athens airport was a very difficult one. He couldn't enter my gate area, and I couldn't enter his. So, we delayed my going to the gate as long as possible. Tearfully I cleared passport control to go to my American Airlines flight bound for London. I was so upset to be leaving him that I sat down at the wrong gate. Until I heard my name paged, I didn't realize this!

I was escorted to the waiting plane that had already boarded. The plane wouldn't have left for London until they found me, due to the fact that I had checked through two suitcases. I was so apologetic, and they were so gracious. Meanwhile, Rich had heard my name paged, and he couldn't find out from anyone what had happened. It would be three days before he heard my version of the incident!

It was hard leaving him again. I realized that I had a long way to travel in front of me, so I composed myself and began to think about his next leave. He would be home at the end of June. This would be after he had been out of the U.S. for nine months. I knew he would be excited to see his home again and all the changes that had been made during the time he was away. I concentrated on thinking about that for the long flights back to South Dakota. I also made myself a mental note and some lists of things that I wanted to get accomplished before his arrival.

 Linda J. Johnson

CHAPTER 29

My flights went surprisingly well, but for Rich it wasn't to be. When he arrived in Dubai, there were no designated personnel waiting for him. He had to take a taxi to the holding hotel. This was money out of his pocket again for the leave. He was already tired and upset about the company's treatment of him initially, and this added to his frustration.

When he finally got back on-site, he filed a complaint describing his experiences. The first response to his complaint was a nasty letter from the man in charge of operations for the company over Dubai. Two weeks after this incident, the number two man in charge of the company in Iraq, the DPM (deputy program manager) visited D-2.

He met with Rich and Chris when he arrived. He understood Rich's position and intervened for him. He gave Rich the rest of the letter and memo, which hadn't been given to Rich in full by the administrator earlier. When Rich was able to read the entire letter, he saw that that the company actually addressed how unfortunate they felt it was that this had happened to him. They also discussed what they were doing to ensure that it didn't happen to any other employee in the future.

During that same visit, Chris was able to give his resume to the DPM for consideration for a promotion. Chris told him that he had been interviewing and hadn't heard back anything on the administration positions he had applied for. The DPM took Chris's resume, and within a month, Chris was promoted. Chris would be moving up north to a B site (Al Asad Air Base).

Rich said it was a tough day when Chris finally left D-2. They had established a closer bond being in that environment together. Rich knew they would probably never be in this type of situation again in their lives. I worried because Chris wouldn't be able to take calls now. There was no cell phone service on that base. So, I would have to wait for him to call from the group phones on his phone cards.

Chris went on to thrive in that environment and was promoted twice after he got up there. Chris's official position became timekeeper for three hundred people. He got his own company e-mail address and personal stateside phone line for use.

Eventually I was able to reach him when he was free in his office. This helped my stress levels tremendously. Chris assured me not to worry because he said that the base there, or site he was transferred to, was very calm in comparison to Baghdad. He said it was sure boring, in fact! He spent lots of extra hours working in his office to pass the time.

While they were both deployed and on two different

bases, the communication would get quite hectic. Sometimes I got a call at 9:00 a.m. from Rich and would get Chris's calls at midnight. That type of schedule filled my days.

During this time, I recall the St. Patrick's Day parade of 2007 held in downtown Sioux Falls. I had never attended a St. Patrick's Day event. A good friend called and asked me to join her for the day.

Imagine my surprise when I saw a group of demonstrators marching in the parade protesting the Iraq war and trashing our president by carrying signs reading things like, "Impeach Bush" or "war criminal" under a picture of President Bush. Something that was supposed to be an innocent outing became very distasteful to me. The experience actually left me emotionally drained and very upset.

To me this is hypocrisy! This group claims to support our troops but not the effort in Iraq. Now, how ridiculous is this? If they are for our military and men deployed but against our president, who is the commander-in-chief and their boss, they are against us personally! Our men, who are military contractors, are directly attacked also because they are attached to the military. Many of our men and women in Iraq feel betrayed by this kind of foolish reasoning.

I was so disturbed by the decision of our city's parade organizers for allowing this to happen. In Colorado Springs, Colorado, that same day, the local police stopped anti-war protestors from marching. This was done out of respect for our people deployed.

Wasn't the St. Patrick's Day parade supposed to be an entertainment venue? Wasn't this for everyone? If so, I wondered what would've happened if some of us in support of our efforts would've marched with placards. Would we be allowed? Would that be a proper venue? I'll never attend another St. Patrick's Day event in this city.

Right before Easter that spring, I also took a quick trip down to Kansas City to see Chris's kids and check up on them. Our ex–daughter-in-law let me stay at her new place. We later learned that she had gotten most of Chris's paychecks out of him throughout his time in Iraq. She had used our grandchildren as an excuse for needing one thing after another.

Much of Chris's money was going her way over and above the child support he already paid to her. It was so wrong. She had led Chris to believe that she was going to get back together with him. This sort of story is going on all over Iraq and everywhere else that we have men deployed who are in conflicted relationships. I did my best to encourage him to plan for a new life after Iraq and move on.

Rich has told me countless stories of relationship after relationship that hadn't been good ahead of a deployment. Although it may be true that absence makes the heart grow fonder, it isn't very likely that a fumbling relationship will improve during a deployment. More often than not, the stories are told of marriages and engagements that go on the rocks.

Rich and I have purchased and sent in many marriage and family books to the men who request them. These guys don't automatically have someone to turn to for emotional or mental support there. They don't have a resident chaplain around watching over them, or anyone else for that matter. Like my husband says, "They just have to tough it out and deal with it." I think he means, "Be a man," whatever that means.

Rich himself was very fortunate in that for the first year

  Linda J. Johnson

while he was in Iraq we taped all of our church services for him and then sent them in to him. He was able to be a part of our Sunday worship. He has regularly attended the Sunday night chapel there on base. It gets to be tricky for him, though, depending upon the site manager. Sometimes they don't get off work in time for him to be at the entire service.

The first chaplain that was at Camp Prosperity was very kind and friendly. He would stop over at the work site and visit with the guys, and Rich would work on his motorcycle. Since then, they have had three others. The second one wasn't as personable, and the third one ran the services right on schedule. This caused Rich to miss out on most of the service, except for the message. There is now a fourth chaplain holding services at the small chapel that Rich attends near D-2. Rich appreciates this new one because he preaches and teaches directly out of the Bible and meets the spiritual needs of the congregants.

As a chaplain myself, I think that those guys might be missing an opportunity for ministry to our men. But I do know that they have their hands full with the army's shortage of chaplains. It is a great void right now and a needed ministry in Iraq.

CHAPTER 30

After I returned from Kansas City in April, I found that water and mud had washed out our backyard. It was spilling down from the spec home built behind our lot. The builder had created a steeper hill in the back that was never planned for that lot, according to what the original plans showed. This lot was causing us runoff and drainage onto our property.

We hadn't yet put in our sod or landscaping around the house, but it was planned for. I called our landscaper and told him about the new hill, and he was as dumbfounded as I was as to why this had been done. I spent the better part of more than four months talking to attorneys here about this situation. No one has wanted to take our case. They were all conflicted, meaning a conflict of interest with our builder. It has been so stressful and very hard on me.

The builder came out to our property for the first time

after that heavy rainstorm and insisted that he hadn't been finished with final grading on our property. I called our city engineers to assist me. They responded by doing a gratuitous lot survey, and then they told us they weren't sure who the fault laid with. I got the distinct impression that either the builders' engineers or city engineers were responsible for this lack of oversight. When I asked them to meet with the builder and me together, they met with him alone while I was gone to Ft. McCoy, Wisconsin. After that they told me that they had done everything that they could and from that point on they wouldn't get involved unless the builder wanted to sit down with us at City Hall. He didn't! It was the usual runaround one might expect from City Hall, but until I encountered it, I wouldn't have believed it!

This has become an ongoing battle with our builder. This is not yet resolved. We have lost a matured spruce tree on our property line in the back, as well as a privacy tree to the north of the house. This is costing us extra money and time, along with a lot of stress and heartache.

I told Rich that I was sure this wouldn't have happened if he was here. In other words, they would probably have come to an agreement with him rather than just not dealing with me. We still haven't come to a final conclusion as to what to do with this issue, but we have completed all the work that we can on the yard. By moving a new tree in to the north closer to the house, the draining issues on that side of the house appear for now to be resolved.

Meanwhile, Rich's fifty-third birthday was coming up, and I wanted to send him something special. My sister Cathy had purchased a kaleidoscope for her husband from

  Linda J. Johnson

New York, and I wanted one for Rich. She had given me the name of the manufacturer. I found one of them in a smaller version online and had it sent to Rich. He later told me that it was such a peaceful gift of light in that place of darkness. It is now home on his dresser because he doesn't want anything to happen to it!

We had contracted the downstairs to my cousin Randy Bruner, of Bruner Construction in Sioux Falls. It was coming along rapidly, and I enjoyed picking out the fixtures, countertop, and carpet for the downstairs. Everything had to be in partnership with Rich by using the Internet. I would find what I thought we should put in, take a digital picture, and send it to him for his approval. He was encouraged to know that this project would be done by the time he got home at the end of June. It was an exciting time for both of us.

I began doing some part-time work for the school district as a substitute teacher. This was a good decision and helped me stay occupied while the builders were in the house.

May brought me to a planning time with our niece Laurie. She was going to host a Fourth of July party at their lake home to honor her parents' fiftieth wedding anniversary and Rich and my wedding anniversary. Rich and I had met thirty years before on the Fourth of July. It would be a special day for us.

Rich's sister Jannie and her husband were going to celebrate their fiftieth anyway in 2007, so we planned to combine the events. Laurie, Jannie, and I spent a few hours getting the invitations written. We planned for decorations and selected the food to be served. It would be a glorious reunion for all of us and a wonderful homecoming for Rich.

For Mother's Day weekend my girlfriend Charlotte

arrived from Colorado. She is from South Dakota originally. She was in Sioux Falls to bury her mother's remains and hold a small funeral. Charlotte had visited us twice on Kauai, and now she was visiting for the second time in South Dakota since Rich had deployed. Her visit was timely because it came at a time when I desperately needed extra moral support due to feeling overwhelmed.

Since February when Rich had returned to Baghdad from Greece, things began to quiet down a lot over there. Slowly the surge began to work, and they noticed fewer bombings and fewer sirens going off. They were no longer sent to bunker or hard surface buildings as often.

It appeared, though, that the insurgents were starting a new tactic. Bridges began blowing up all over Baghdad. The enemies of our mission were trying to isolate neighborhoods and cut them off.

Right after Chris transferred up north, an explosion occurred nearby to the working site of our men. In fact, it happened so close that our administrator was able to get pictures by climbing up on a pole to snap them. There were Iraqi police everywhere. I have these pictures that he sent to me, and they are frightening!

When I looked at the pictures of Rich running in front of the smoke and clouds of debris, I almost fainted. I maybe needed to see those, and then again, maybe I didn't! We are so thankful that this incident didn't cost us any of our men's lives. It really brought the reality of the danger they are in daily, closer to home for me.

As our troops cleared Baghdad in 2007, everything calmed down neighborhood by neighborhood. It stayed very

  Linda J. Johnson

peaceful and calm most of the year. This fact had allowed both Rich and me to relax somewhat and to not be so worried for his personal safety.

For Chris, well, I knew he was okay. He did send some fantastic pictures of a sandstorm coming upon their base. They were so incredible. Chris was thoroughly reveling in his job and his position with the company. We had some really good phone conversations while he was up there. He was so proud of the job he was doing. He seemed relatively happy for the first time in his short life.

For me, having two of them in two different places posed some new and unique problems! It seemed that I was now playing double duty with two guys calling or e-mailing at any time of the day or night. Rich would get a hold of me in the morning, and then Chris would call just as I was calling it quits for the day. The support that they needed was constant. I know how important it was for them to get through to me and to have someone behind them while they were deployed. It always seemed like I was doing paperwork for one or the other! I was making phone calls regularly for Chris to straighten out some of his personal matters as well.

Another project on my plate for 2007 was the wedding ceremony of my niece Katie. I was asked to officiate for her wedding coming up in July, to be held just a week after Rich would go back to Iraq. So, I worked on the service and wanted to have everything ready before working on Rich's next leave and the planning for that.

Also, I had two graduation events to attend in Colorado at the end of May. I had never gotten to attend any of the high school graduation ceremonies for my youngest sister's daughters, and now I would. All of these activities seemed to fill in time for me between Rich's leaves. It was nice to visit with family and dear friends once again. Any break at that time from the house issues was welcomed by me!

Looking back at the first half of 2007, I think it flew by. I never seemed to have a moment to myself, and yet, this was good. Again, the objective for me was to fill up time until he could come home again.

Fortunately, Rich's sister Ruth and her husband, Roy, from Flandreau, South Dakota, were always calling me and encouraging me during this timeframe. They would phone whenever they came into Sioux Falls. Then they would stop over and pick me up. We would do errands together. I have enjoyed renewing our family ties with them. We were very close when our kids were all young. This was during the first nine years of our marriage when we lived in South Dakota.

Ruth had called to check on me regularly, and she didn't forget to ask about Rich. She always wanted to hear how he was doing. I look forward to the day when we can get back to double dating on a permanent basis. Then I won't have to be the "odd man out"!

If I haven't said it enough, the support of my husband's family has been awesome. They are always there for me, if I need them, and that support leaves me with a feeling of peace and security.

CHAPTER 31

During the second half of 2007, the media seemed to begin to put emphasis on and feature those who were negative towards the war effort. On the one hand, I wasn't seeing as many pictures of fallen soldiers in the Army Times, which would indicate we were progressing militarily, but on the other hand, the press continued to keep up the negative barrage.

Another thing I couldn't understand was why the story of our men and their lives or loss of lives wasn't published anywhere. Our human toll isn't in the total figures for Americans who lose their lives in Iraq or Afghanistan. It's as if it doesn't happen, yet it does!

We support our military 100%, and yet, we aren't given the respect and consideration for the effort and service of our loved ones.

It appears that we will always be behind the scenes and

misunderstood. Yet, our families are solid in support of the president's efforts and absolutely committed to the troops. We send our loved ones to work with them. We sacrifice also for this global cause against terrorism.

In fact, I might add that our American dollars are occasionally spent in Iraq on items for our homes and for gifts to others. Our loved ones purchase from Iraqi businesspeople, thus helping out in the economic recovery of the country. This is in addition to working in the training of Iraqis and the rebuilding of Iraq.

Now, I'm not mentioning wasteful spending here or commenting on misrepresentation that the media has tried to spin many times. The idea that America's defense dollars are wasted in Iraq to me is ridiculous! I'm speaking of discretionary dollars that our men spend on items that can be purchased at local Iraqi shops. This has kept many an Iraqi family who is still living in the country afloat.

In my heart, I actually don't believe Americans in general understand that our men receive their pay in U.S. bank accounts. Those dollars are coming home to America and spent back in our own economy. In my opinion, our paychecks are a part of what has kept the American economy afloat in the past few years. Due to the combat zone pay and exclusion of paying taxes on the first $82,500 annual income, the refund checks from IRS come back home to America also. Those dollars are spent here, stateside.

It would be interesting to get a real head count of Americans working in Iraq and Afghanistan at any given time. If we would just stop and estimate that at an average wage of $80,000 annually paid for every man and woman

  Linda J. Johnson

deployed to Iraq, then we might have a better understanding of just how important that payroll is that is coming back into America. It's not lost money. I believe some in the media would have us believe that.

If our men ever get paid the back pay that I believe they are owed for working overtime every day while in Iraq, then an even larger amount of dollars will pour back into our economy. Rich has never been paid overtime for his working twelve hours a day every day. His paychecks only include the regular pay hours for a twelve-hour day. I know that there is a lawsuit pending against the company that holds the contract to pay those overtime hours, and we are praying and hoping one day we will receive this back pay.

Do our troops and our men not have the right to be paid for their jobs? Do we have the right to criticize their choice of vocation? Do we have the right to do this so viciously? Only history will tell us how important the efforts in Iraq and Afghanistan have been overall.

This is what our loved ones and our military have chosen to do. I don't get that people don't get that. One would have to separate payroll out of spending dollars that are spent on reconstruction inside Iraq, for Iraq only, to do a fair comparison or a fair critique.

The political candidates and race of 2008 had started out with candidates focused on Iraq ahead of the country's economic meltdown. It turned into a conglomeration of accusations between congressional delegates, parties, and candidates as to just how Americans' monies were being squandered, and an immediate finger-pointing began. All of this was carried on by campaigns that were spending a record-breaking amount of money to get elected to our White House, in the guise of representing us! Meanwhile, our deployed men and women sank into the background.

Rich has told me many times this past year, during the campaign for the White House, to turn off the news and relax. He reported that on base everyone kept their opinions mainly to themselves and didn't engage in divisive politics. All of them who wanted to vote absentee were able to do so successfully this year. Rich has been able to ignore the politics of the past year and simply turn it off in order to keep his head clear.

The thing I keep asking myself is why in the world would any American hold other Americans who are in Iraq in contempt? Both Rich and I cannot believe that Americans stateside are very ignorant of the potential danger to them that radical Islam poses. We don't understand just why we would pit ourselves against one another at a time when our efforts should be united to stamp out terrorism worldwide.

By just looking at the capabilities list surmised from the 9/11 commission report, as summarized in the book, "The 9/11 report, a Graphic Adaptation," any American who "lets down their guard" in a post 9/11 world should read this book in its entirety.

Capabilities summary 9/11 Report:

- The commission was struck by the narrow and unimaginative menu of options for actions offered to both Presidents Clinton and Bush.
- Before 9/11 the U.S. tried to solve the Al Qaeda problem with the same institutions and capabilities

  Linda J. Johnson

it used in the last stages of the Cold War. These were insufficient and little was done to expand options.

- Both defense secretaries Cohen and Rumsfeld gave their principal attention to other challenges.
- The FAA's capabilities to take aggressive anticipatory security measures were especially weak.
- The FAA could have expanded no-fly lists, searched passengers identified by the CAPP's screening system, deployed federal air marshals domestically, strengthened cockpit doors, and alerted air crews to a different kind of hijacking than they had been trained to expect.
- Government agencies are often passive, accepting what they view as givens, including that efforts to identify and fix glaring vulnerabilities to dangerous threats would be too costly, too controversial, or too disruptive.
- The FBI did not have the capability to link the collective knowledge of agents in the field to national priorities. The acting director did not learn of the bureau's hunt for two possible Al Qaeda operatives or the arrest of an Islamic extremist taking flight training until 9/11.
- *At no point before 9/11 was the Department of Defense fully engaged in countering Al Qaeda, though it was perhaps the most dangerous foreign enemy threatening the U.S[1]

More importantly, the mission of Al Qaeda as stated in "Army releases captured war terror documents…" should capture the attention of us all.

There were many portions of the Quran quoted in these documents as well, possibly as justification for terrorist actions.

Al Qaeda's statement of purpose (equivalent to a mission statement):

"A religious group of the nation of Mohammad (God's blessing and peace be upon him) whose faith is the faith of the believers in Sunna (profit teachings) and Jama'ah (consensus), are adopting Jihad as a method for change so that the 'Word of God' becomes supreme, and they (the group) are working to provoke Jihad, prepare for it, and exercise it by whatever means possible."

The prophet said, "There are those of my nation who are victorious and will stay victorious till the day they face their fate and die" narrated by (Al-Bukhari 252/4). And the prophet also said: "There is still a group of my nation fighting for justice victorious over their enemy until the last of them fights the Antichrist" narrated by Abu Daud (The book of Jihad, Chapter 4) [2]

I probably don't need to define the word jihad, but I will. It is "a Muslim holy war or spiritual struggle against infidels." The infidels spoken about here are all non-Muslims.

This Iraq mission in our viewpoint is very important to the future security of our nation. It's as simple as that. Each of our loved ones plays a vital role towards the success of stabilizing the Middle East. Iraq and Afghanistan are the front lines. It's not rocket science to stand together as a nation. It is common sense during a time of war!

I'm not really sure if the guy on the street understands what a negative rebound effect an immediate pullout from Iraq would cause for America. Besides having a negative

  Linda J. Johnson

impact on the morale of our military and those deployed, we would face millions of payroll dollars not coming home to cities and towns across America as people would demobilize.

A rash act like this may have many negative ramifications on local unemployment figures. There would be so many men looking for jobs here at home. It will be mind-boggling if this happens.

Recently, we have seen increased violence in and around Baghdad, as the Iraqi parliament was engaging in discussions to renew our U.S. security agreement, which allows our forces to stay inside Iraq up to the year 2011. I believe the violence inside Iraq would increase astronomically with broadcasting or publishing a withdrawal timetable of Americans from this country.

What would happen to all those local people and Iraqis who have worked with the coalition forces and want a democratic form of government there? I firmly believe that many of our military and loved ones working with them will feel that their being there was in vain and that we will continue to have a divided country on any decision made in haste.

I think John McCain said it best in portions of an article he wrote while campaigning for the presidency. We wholeheartedly agree with his assessment.

We must win Iraq war, and not just withdraw

In January 2007, when Gen. David Petraeus took command in Iraq, he called the situation "hard" but not "hopeless." Today, 18 months later, violence has fallen by up to 80 percent to the lowest levels in four years, and Sunni and Shiite terrorists are reeling from a string of defeats. The situation now is full of hope, but considerable hard work remains to consolidate our fragile gains ...

Perhaps he (Obama) is unaware that the U.S. Embassy in Baghdad has recently certified that, as one news article put it, "Iraq has met all but three of 18 original benchmarks set by Congress last year to measure security, political and economic progress." Even more heartening has been progress that's not measured by the benchmarks. More than 90,000 Iraqis, many of them Sunnis who once fought against the government, have signed up as Sons of Iraq to fight against the terrorists. Nor do they measure Prime Minister Nouri al-Maliki's newfound willingness to crack down on Shiite extremists in Basra and Sadr City—actions that have done much to dispel suspicions of sectarianism.

The success of the surge has not changed Obama's determination to pull out all of our combat troops. All that has changed is his rationale. In a recent New York Times op-ed and a speech, he offered his "plan for Iraq" in advance of his first "fact finding" trip to that country in more than three years. It consisted of the same old proposal to pull all of our troops out within 16 months. In 2007 he wanted to withdraw because he thought the war was lost. If we had taken his advice, it would have been. Now he wants to withdraw because he thinks Iraqis no longer need our assistance ...

But I have also said that any draw-downs must be based on a realistic assessment of conditions on the ground, not on an artificial timetable crafted for domestic political reasons. This is the crux of my

  Linda J. Johnson

disagreement with Obama…

The danger is that extremists supported by al-Qaida and Iran could stage a comeback, as they have in the past when we've had too few troops in Iraq.

Obama seems to have learned nothing from recent history. I find it ironic that he is emulating the worst mistake of the Bush administration by waving the "Mission Accomplished" banner prematurely.

I am also dismayed that he never talks about winning the war—only of ending it. But if we don't win the war, our enemies will. A triumph for the terrorists would be a disaster for us. That is something I will not allow to happen as president. Instead I will continue implementing a proven counterinsurgency strategy not only in Iraq but also in Afghanistan, with the goal of creating stable, secure, self-sustaining democratic allies.[3]

CHAPTER 32

Meanwhile, I got busy planning for Rich's homecoming at the end of June. I really wanted the house to be just like new for him.

Chris had requested and was not given a special leave to come home for the Fourth of July. We knew he wouldn't be with us for our party. It was always so hard with Rich and Chris split up now and stationed in two different places. Chris could be transferred to within four miles of his dad when he was leaving for the states, but he couldn't get to his dad. While in Iraq, they may as well have been continents apart if they weren't on the same base.

I often commented that year that I was going to fly in there to check this entire situation out. Both Rich and Chris would give me an emphatic, "No way!" Rich has always added,

"I never want you to come here." His response makes me more anxious about what is going on in there than I want to be!

Meanwhile, back on-site, Rich was picking up mixed signals from his site manager about putting in for promotions. Every time Rich tried to interview or apply for a new position, the site manager would talk him out of it.

At this point Rich had received many medals and awards from the company and army groups, along with other coalition units he worked with. I felt that I wanted to do something special with them to honor him.

My cousin had built in a special recessed, lighted wall in our downstairs to display the memorabilia. I decided that I wanted to create a shadow box display for Rich as a thirtieth wedding anniversary gift from me. This project took several meetings with a local artist.

After choosing the frames and mats and finalizing my choices, the end result was a very tasteful and unique presentation depicting his achievements, successes, and awards for his first two years in Iraq! I had this completed prior to his getting home.

The following is a quote from an e-mail I received from the Assistant Deputy Project Manager in Iraq when he viewed the digital photos I sent to him of the display.

> Mrs. Johnson:
> What you have done for Richard is highly commendable, and I am sure he will be totally surprised when he sees the awards displayed so professionally. Richard continuously sets the standard, and is one of our most dedicated employees serving our military customer, with the best quality

Linda J. Johnson

equipment to conduct their mission.

We are proud to have Richard on our Lear Siegler team. Thanks for sharing this most positive tribute to a most deserving husband.[1]

During the time that this was going on, we had another curveball thrown at us. Delta Airlines had made a flight change to Rich's upcoming trip home. He wouldn't have enough connection time in either New York (JFK) or Cincinnati, Ohio, to connect with his Sioux Falls flight. I was scrambling on this end to fix this problem.

We had already charged this ticket three months ahead of his leave to ensure that he got those requested dates off. His site manager had told him that he had to purchase a new ticket if he wanted to change through another connecting city (Atlanta). Rich thought they would reissue the ticket and then credit our card for the first ticket. I remember telling him that it didn't sound right. We had enough money inside the travel agency that LSI used, that they could just refund our card and reissue a new ticket with the same money.

I called Delta Airlines corporate offices and asked them to assist us because our credit card was charged a second time. Delta said of course they would honor his request for an itinerary change and cancel the old ticket. However, they were blocked from doing this because the travel agency that the company used wouldn't issue a credit. In fact, the travel agency was telling Rich after he handed over his card a second time for the same leave, that now he would pay a penalty and forfeit part of the money. They cited Delta as not willing to reimburse them for the portion changed. Delta totally denied this and assisted us.

It took me three days and many, many phone calls and e-mails to get this straightened out. This problem went all the way to the corporate offices in Iraq, but to no avail. Once again I didn't have anyone within the company to help me handle this. We now had almost $5,000 tied up in credit card charges with the travel agency. We would be stuck with the interest charges and the hassle until it got straightened out.

We ended up having to put a dispute on our credit card and provide the e-mails and other proofs in order to get our own money placed back in our account! I began to wonder why the company's huge administrative staff somewhere in Iraq couldn't intervene and solve the problem. We shouldn't have had to spend the time and effort on untangling these problems ourselves without assistance.

For me it appeared that our men were given last priority instead of first priority. Yet, I knew that the most important people over there for the company were the men on the front lines and those who worked daily with our customer, the military. It didn't make any sense. Today the company has three times the number of personnel on the administration roster than the number they had when Rich was first deployed. It would appear that position after position is created in the administration offices. I believe that these people should be there to assist our mechanics.

I have spent many a tearful day and night over this reality. Our men appear to be disposable and don't have many rights or advocates even in their own company. It's unfair at best and deplorable at worst.

  Linda J. Johnson

Rich told me that the only way he survives there is to mind his own business. He says he just does his job and keeps his mouth shut. He has always said that like anywhere else, cronyism rules in Iraq among military contracting companies. It's who you know and how well you talk a good game, as opposed to what you know.

He and Chris have both seen surprising personnel decisions made in Iraq, including promotions and firings, at the whim of a single site manager or person who can work the system. Many in management utilize paperwork to get anyone in or out of their jobs. These can be people who have never managed personnel in the past.

We have seen that stateside recruiters and company HR personnel get moved to Iraq and placed into six-figure income jobs. This happened regularly. The administration employees or office personnel list keeps growing every time Rich comes home on leave. New jobs appear to be created for positions above the mechanics and master mechanics.

I mentioned that there really is no place and no organization that works with us in this country. The families of American contractors who are left behind stand on their own. Any contacts with organizations that I have made through searching online haven't resulted in any long-term support. There have been some attempts to help out contractors who have problems with their previous employers; however, the vast majority and their families are left on their own with no place to turn for moral support. I fear that we will have many, many families affected in the near future as jobs become scarce in Iraq and men are sent back home to this unstable economy.

We want to put a human face to the silent majority of families who have been or are deployed on behalf of Iraqi freedom. We want and desire a positive reflection for our efforts and the service of our loved ones. It was heartbreaking to watch the news feature stories about the 4,000th military casualty in Iraq, but no mention was made of American contractors' deaths. It is as if their sacrifices didn't count.

Rich and I are, and have been, fully supportive of President George W. Bush's Iraq policy, and we don't believe in a troop withdrawal timetable. We do believe that our men and our families need to be included in these decisions and be made aware of future plans regarding our presence in Iraq or Afghanistan. All persons actually involved in the effort need to be heard and be a part of the planning.

  Linda J. Johnson

CHAPTER 33

Right before Rich got home in the summer of 2007, I responded to an U.S. Army Times editorial. A letter had been written and published in the Army Times in June and included some of the following:

> How do you think a soldier feels when he works side by side with people who are making, in one month, the average private's yearly salary? It doesn't matter if they work for a contractor or not. The contract is paid by the U.S. government. Outside contractors do the same job as some soldiers, but they are paid enormous amounts more. There have been 393 contractors killed, according to figures compiled by Iraq Coalition Casualty Count at: http://icasualties.org, compared with 3,388 U.S. troops, as of May 17, 2007, according

to the Defense Dept. The American soldier is being taken advantage of. Jennifer Parker, civilian

Bellingham, Wash.[1]

The *Army Times* contacted me after I sent in a response to this letter. They published my rebuttal letter as a response to the above. The *Army Times* has been very supportive and understanding of the roles that civilian/military contractors play in OIF and OEF.

This was my response:

As a proud wife of an Army contractor, who is serving in Baghdad, I take objection to the letter by Jennifer Parker ("Contractors profit," June 4).

As to working side by side, they do in fact, work side by side, and enjoy, for the most part, a very amiable and good working relationship in the most dangerous part of the world today. They work together as comrades and hold no ill will towards each other. They need each other, in fact, to get the job done.

It sounds nice to say outside contractors make this much money; however, it is far from reality. I know my husband's pay since August, 2005, when he deployed to Iraq, has stayed almost the same, and he is paid in conjunction with Army pay levels.

Why does he do it? He is from a military family, and he could finally do his part this way.

I say let us support one and all who are deployed in harm's way today, and remember all those left behind, who wait for them to come home.

Linda J Johnson, civilian

Sioux Falls, S.D[2]

    Linda J. Johnson

When Rich got home, he was so proud of me again. We e-mailed the article to Iraq. Again, the company was very pleased with *Army Times*. The company spends a lot of time and effort in stabilizing and attempting to improve relationships between our men and the military they serve. I received a lot of thank-you notes by e-mail from wives of contractors who viewed the article. I have a passion for setting things right regarding the role of our men in Iraq. We want the American public to know the facts and develop a better appreciation for our loved ones and their roles there, at this time of war.

One of the first visits we received during the summer of 2007 was from my cousin, U.S. Naval Commander Tommy Simpson, and his family, of San Diego, California. Tommy has often commented that this has been a strange twist of affairs for him to be an encouragement for the civilian (Rich) deployed, when it is usually the other way around! He and his dad, my father's only living brother, and their extended family, have been very kind to me and good to Rich throughout this ordeal.

They don't forget him on his birthday or holidays, and they have tried to make special time to spend with us when he is home. They are usually also there for me when I need them. They live only half a mile away!

The weather cooperated for Rich's fifth leave. He had only seen his home once when it was brand new, and now we had the yard in and the landscaping completed. The downstairs was also done, and almost everything was completed for him. I even hired professional house cleaners, complete with an outside window cleaner, to have everything appear just like new! Rich always comments that when he walks in, the house still smells like a brand-new home. He is so thrilled with that.

For this fifth leave, he would be in for fourteen days, and it seemed way too short! His arrival on June 25 was so awesome. I was so happy that he was so pleased with everything done inside the house and with the yard. The only blip on the radar screen for us right then was that we couldn't get our builder to accept any responsibility for the drainage problems we were having in the backyard. I didn't want Rich to get upset and have it out with this guy while he was on such a short leave. We conceded our defeat for the meantime.

Rich was scheduled for a routine endoscopy while home. He had a full day of tests done and dental appointments to squeeze in his limited time. This is again routine for us while he is in. So far our providers have been very cooperative with me in getting Rich scheduled and in when he needs to during his leave dates.

Rich even has his own stylist in a local hair shop who will schedule his haircut for him when he gets here. This is one small but very important necessity that brings him a step closer toward being normal while he is home.

After Rich gets over jet lag, I give him some lists of chores to accomplish while he is here. These are also designed to help him feel like a part of everything going on around the house. It always takes him a few days to get into routine.

One highlight for that leave was a double date with Rich's sister Ruth and her husband, Roy. Finally we could all go out together for dinner and be well, "normal." I keep using that word; however, I don't know how else to explain what it is like to live a long-distance marriage. We attempt to recon-

  Linda J. Johnson

nect during his leaves and maintain normalcy as much as possible for his sake and mine!

I keep pictures taken during all of his leaves and send him copies or e-mail them to his memory stick. He now has a digital frame in his living quarters so he can have memories and family with him all of the time.

Of course, the most important event of that summer leave, for us, would be the Fourth of July anniversary party at the lake home of Rich's niece.

It turned out to be a beautiful day, and one of Rich's brothers from Idaho drove in for the event. We had lots of family and some friends attend. What a wonderful Independence Day, for many reasons. There was plenty of food, and when the day ended, we agreed to host Rich's brothers and sisters who were there at our house the next day. We would all be sorting through old family photos and picking out those we wanted copies of.

Laurie sent us home with lots of food to serve. Rich and I reminisced that night over the past thirty years. It appeared to us that we were more than blessed despite the hardship of this separation while he worked inside Iraq.

That evening, as Rich fell asleep in his easy chair watching TV, something very strange happened. We were awaiting the fireworks display from our county fairgrounds. We can see these clearly from our back deck.

About 10:00 p.m., someone in our neighborhood set off their own fireworks. The noise and blast startled Rich. I watched him jump out of his chair and pace the back deck. "Why are those people aiming at our house?" he asked me. He was really jumpy, and this was not a typical reaction from him. Rich has always been mellow and cool-headed in almost every situation.

All of a sudden, I realized that Iraq was never far away from his thoughts. As he had peacefully fallen asleep, the fireworks' blasts brought Iraq right there to him in Sioux Falls. It didn't help that he couldn't see into the darkness. He couldn't tell who was shooting them off or where they were. It's very dark out here at night in this subdivision. This incident spooked us both.

I shut the house up and turned the AC on. I figured he wouldn't be able to hear everything as well. He did fall back asleep finally after midnight, when all the fireworks displays were done.

One of the last events that Rich and I attended was a school reunion for those students who had attended a one-room schoolhouse in Ward, South Dakota. Two of Rich's sisters and a brother were also there for the event. This was held on a hot July day, and Rich got to reconnect with some old friends. Everyone congratulated him on his achievements and work in Iraq. They were very proud of him. It was a nice event to attend ahead of his leaving for Iraq.

Another thing that happened during that leave was that he had a scheduled conference call and interview for the master mechanic position at his site. His administrator called ahead of the interview and told him what to prepare for. Other guys had already finished interviewing over in Iraq, and Rich would be called in the middle of the night here! He stayed awake and felt prepared for the interview.

We were both excited for this and really believed that Rich would get this promotion, finally! After all, he had always been the backup for the QAQC (quality control technician), and he had filled in for the foreman on more than one occasion. His interview went really well, and we actually thought he had it in the bag. Little did he know he would not get chosen then because his own site manager at the time played favorites and chose someone else! In fact, Rich was shocked, and it was very hard for him to go back to Iraq knowing the job had been given to a man of lesser seniority and possibly less experience. I had to work hard to encourage and remind him that everything was in God's perfect timing!

One thing about my husband that is different from me is that he is a man of peace and doesn't confront people instantly. He went back holding up his head. In less than four months, the same man who got the promotion would be gone, along with the site manager. It was, in fact, God's perfect timing, because Rich never wanted to change sites. He wanted to receive the promotion on his own base.

Rich left on a Sunday afternoon for Iraq, and I left for Montana the following Wednesday to officiate at a July wedding ceremony for my niece. This would be a four-day event, and I was glad to have it on the calendar to fill in the time. The days after he leaves are the worst. I must readjust again to not having him home. So this time, I wouldn't have time to sit around and mope!

CHAPTER 34

At the same time I was in Montana, a letter was published in our Sioux Falls newspaper, the Argus Leader. The title of the letter read, "Civilians in Iraq for money." The only reason I knew about this was that my brother-in-law saved it for me and told me about it when I got back. He believed it was in direct reference to the letter I had had published in the Army Times the week before.

When I finally got to read it, I was shocked and saddened all at the same time! By publishing such a letter, our local newspaper was actually stirring up the pot to cause a controversy! It appeared to me that they didn't bother to check out the entire story before publishing the following letter.

I read a letter submitted by a civilian from Sioux Falls to the Stars & Stripes military newspaper that is read by thousands of troops worldwide. I am from Sturgis and currently in Iraq, so the writer hit close to home.

She spoke of a topic that most troops get heated about, even when reading it. Let me advise you that nowhere does it say that civilians have to come to Iraq to do our job.

We are soldiers, and proud to serve our country, but civilians are taking it from us. We see them on our forward operating bases wearing our uniforms (improperly) and collecting paychecks with which we only can imagine to do what. Then, we have to hear about them, Not getting to wear the uniform," or, "well my spouse is in Iraq, too."

The reason they don't get to wear the uniform is because they obviously don't stand for the same thing a soldier does. The uniform is the only things we have here to display our pride for the USA.

Civilians don't seem to be here for the same reason. The ones I talk to are here for the money, and the free travel that they get, far more than we do.

A 15 month deployment gives us 15 days with family once. A 15-month voluntary temporary duty gives them more than 15 days of R and R every four months. Definitely not fair.

The next time someone wants to rant and rave about a spouse over here, put them in check and tell them, if they weren't greedy for the glory they think it gives them, they wouldn't be.

Sgt. Amber S. Fitz
Sturgis[1]

I immediately wrote to the *Argus Leader* on July 19, 2007. I wanted to know why. Why did our hometown newspaper

Linda J. Johnson

publish such a letter without checking out the original letter from the gal who first wrote into *Army Times* and then check on my published letter in the *Army Times* before publishing a letter from Sergeant Fitz? The following is my letter to the *Argus Leader*:

TO ARGUS LEADER VOICES

Just got home from Montana (where I officiated at a wedding), and then today, a relative handed me last Saturday's Argus leader Voice of the People page; July 14, 2007

I do believe that Ms. Fitz is referring to my letter that was published by Army Times on July 2, 2007. I didn't know it went out to Stars and Stripes. The initial letter from Ms. Parker that I responded to, and the Army Times contacted ME to publish my response is also being faxed to you for your review.

I guess my question to all of you would be WHY? To question Mrs Fitz, well, I won't do that, because she is deployed, and deserves all the support she can get. The why is as to WHY is the Argus Leader publishing Ms Fitz response in this newspaper when Ms Fitz could respond to my letter in the Army Times, if she so desired, and if they wanted to publish it. Furthermore, she could contact me, if she read the article, because my name and city was published, if she wanted to debate this issue WITH ME, she could've found me easily in this day and age.

If this is the Voice of the People, then do my husband (who is deployed as an Army contractor) and my son, (who is deployed as an Army contractor, and is separated from service, but chose to go back this way to Iraq) and ME, a family member left behind, count? What I mean is, do our voices and opinions count? Or, is the Argus Leader deciding to "spin" the role of thousands of Americans working as contractors in a war zone, and deciding that they are all there for the money? If that is the case, is anyone in Iraq not being paid? We have an all volunteer military right now too, so, end of argument.

As far as ranting and raving, please let me know if you think the Army Times would publish a letter that is ranting and raving. That is simply not their style, In fact, it was very good for morale of all deployed, who are working, for the most part, side by side. While Ms. Fitz is entitled to her opinion, she must remember that 70% of all military contractors called back to Iraq, are vets, so therefore, she is criticizing her own, so to speak.

For me, I am the daughter of a vet, born a South Dakotan, and true blue to the USA. The rest speaks for itself. I repeat, let us support all of those deployed in harms' way, and remember those left behind, and pray for the safe return of all.

Rev. Linda J Johnson
Community services chaplain
Sioux Falls, SD

What really bothered me about the letter from Sergeant Fitz was the note on "free" travel! We, as families of military contractors deployed, pay as much as 55 % of the cost of our airline tickets, to the tune of $1,000 or more. Furthermore, our men work twelve hour days- seven days a week, and military personnel who are deployed get days off inside the war zone (or downtime). I do also know that many, many of our troops get their R and R travel paid for. Their expenses and transport in and out of Iraq for leave are not out-of-pocket expenses like ours is. I am in no way discounting the extra danger they are in, nor am I not in awe of their bravery. We have had many family members deployed as active military, and we have been in full support of them.

I sent all the supporting documents to the *Argus Leader* newspaper. The editors phoned me and asked for permission to publish my letter to them. I told them, "Yes, but only if you will publish the entire scenario, including Ms. Parker's first letter to *Army Times* and the *Army Times* response with my published letter, and then your letter from Sergeant Fitz." I told them to then let the public decide as to what was actually going on and form their own opinion after they saw all the details and correspondence.

They declined, saying they didn't know if they could devote that much space! I told them I would not agree to attack a soldier in public without the entire history of all the letters being published. Of course, the *Argus Leader* would've then been shown to be spinning a topic for effect. This is what it appeared to be to me, anyway.

This newspaper, in my opinion, walks a fine line now with their Iraq reporting. This local newspaper has not been interested much in finding out the real stories behind military contractors' roles in OIF (Operation Iraqi Freedom), OEF (Operation Enduring Freedom), or much about their families. They continue to report on South Dakota peace and justice groups and their meetings, yet I don't really believe that there are a lot of people interested in publicly opposing the war and standing against those involved here in South

Dakota. Our state has one of the highest levels of participation and sacrifice in Operation Iraqi Freedom for military across the nation. We can only guess at the "real" numbers when contractors are included.

Military Statistics > *Iraqi War Casualties (per capita) (most recent) by state*

#5   <u>South Dakota</u>:   2.191 per 100,000 people [2]

> VFA has confirmed that the following states have deployed (or will soon deploy) more troops to Iraq and/or Afghanistan than to any war since World War II: Alaska, Arizona, Delaware, Florida, Georgia, Hawaii, Illinois, Indiana, Kentucky, Louisiana, Maine, Maryland, Massachusetts, Michigan, Minnesota, Mississippi, Missouri, Montana, Nebraska, New Hampshire, New Jersey, New Mexico, New York, North Carolina, Ohio, Oregon, Pennsylvania, Rhode Island, South Carolina, South Dakota, Tennessee, Texas, Vermont, Washington, and Wisconsin.
>
> (from archives Veterans for America, 2008)[3]

On the other hand, the *Minneapolis Star and Tribune* has done a very good job on attempting to report about the involvement of our contracting families in this war. They began working on a story about any Minnesotans or those who had ties to Minnesota who were deployed to Iraq. Rich was born in Pipestone, Minnesota, but raised in South Dakota from the age of four, and still has close family members living there.

A reporter by the name of Jon Tevlin called me back for feedback while I was at Lake Okoboji, Iowa, visiting

  Linda J. Johnson

longtime family friends. We arranged for him to speak to Rich directly from Iraq. Rich called him at a pre-arranged time, and the article came out on August 12, 2007, in the *Minneapolis Star and Tribune*.

This reporter did a very good job on the article. He showed support, concern, and compassion in the way that he presented contractors' stories. It was one of the best up close and personal glimpses into some scenarios of contractors' lives. We were very appreciative to have had an honest article published for once by the media.

An aunt of Rich's later told us that she had read it when her daughter brought the story to her from the Minneapolis newspaper. To me this was bittersweet justice for us after the Argus Leader incident. The portion of this article featuring Rich read:

> … When he was last home in Sioux Falls, S.D., a few days before July 4th, Rich Johnson was snoozing in an easy chair when a neighbor set off some fireworks.
>
> Now, almost two years into his stint as a mechanic in Baghdad's Green Zone, Johnson jumped from his chair, ran out to the yard, and started pacing the deck.
>
> "It was so unlike him," said his wife, Linda. "He's usually so mellow."
>
> The Johnsons had been missionaries, so they are used to living in challenging locations. But, they'd seen nothing like Iraq, where both Rich Johnson, and his son, Chris, are working.
>
> Linda Johnson said she worries about both "24–7," but talks to them daily. People accuse the Johnsons of doing it for the money, but Linda said her husband could make almost as much at home.

"They need him there," she said. "And, we believe we have a vested interest in the global political situation."

In a recent phone call from Baghdad's Green Zone, Rich Johnson said he was proud of the work he and his son were doing. He misses his family terribly, but said the soldiers "really seem to appreciate what we're doing. I'm glad I stepped out and did this. I don't regret any of it."

Right now, he's considering signing up for a third year in Iraq.

Jon Tevlin 612/673–1702[4]

The entire article was done as a tribute to include those who had worked alongside troops in Iraq. Minnesota was welcoming home an unit of military men, and this newspaper wanted to include contractors.

At the end of that summer, the first of two of our natural spruce trees began to die. I had to deal with this by myself and make some more decisions on how to solve another big problem. Sometimes these problems came up so fast and loomed so big that I felt like Rich was the fortunate one! At least he had a routine, and he knew basically each day what to do and what to expect. He also had his needs met for him and people to do his laundry, feed him, and house him! He could focus on his "mission."

We both realized that he was sheltered from daily living and all of these everyday problems. I wanted this for him, on the other hand, because I knew how hard it was for him to be away from home. He was working long hours in extreme conditions. So, this bittersweet reality has become our life.

My "mission to him" is to keep his life as simple as pos-

  Linda J. Johnson

sible and pick up the slack where I can with assisting him to do his job. When he needs something, I send it, or I get it sent to him. We even have retailers like Sears who ship to him directly solving my problem of having to go and purchase, come home and prepare a shipment, and then go to the post office to get it sent!

On a more positive note, in the middle of all the trials with the house and yard that summer, I had befriended a single gal who lived on the block whose brother was killed in Iraq in 2006. While I was complaining about my trials and tribulations regarding having a loved one deployed and having to deal with everything, she was silently listening and wishing she still had that same set of problems. My hearts goes out to her whenever we talk. She is, of course, still grieving the sudden death of her brother, who was active military.

She was able to visit with Rich during that summer of his 2007 leave. Some of the things he could tell her about what could've happened when her brother's vehicle exploded from an IED comforted her. She was one of the first people to whom I showed Rich's medals and awards. She will always say, "We need every person doing whatever they can to complete our mission in Iraq." She has a great deal of respect for Rich and his work there. She always asks me how he is when I visit with her. I watch as she displays her American flag, and she will ask about Rich when mine is out.

She was able to purchase her house through part of the death benefits she received when her brother was killed. Her home honors his sacrifice. I pray that our family will not have to go through that ultimate sacrifice.

CHAPTER 35

Meanwhile, problems were brewing for Chris in Iraq. On his base, there were a lot of personnel changes that summer. A new site manager came in, and to Chris, it appeared that the guy didn't like or appreciate Chris in his job as timekeeper. In fact, the guy was immediately mentioning to Chris, that usually the timekeeper on-site would be a female. Chris didn't give this too much concern but appeared to butt heads with the guy from early on. Chris's reporting structure was to corporate regarding payroll, yet he had to balance orders from this man.

Chris was also having family problems back in Kansas City and was trying to get back on his feet from that acrimonious divorce. He talked to his kids regularly and had planned to see them the first week of September. Chris was approaching his contract renewal date.

He renewed the contract for another year and then put in

for his twenty-one-day leave. Chris had been putting in many extra hours every day and was so proud of his accomplishments with the company. He always tells it like it is. I know about Chris's honesty, and I also know about his dedication. Chris was finally fully supporting his children and was able to give them extras. He had saved up for a down payment to buy a vehicle and was trying to get his credit back in line.

Chris had taken such a beating with his finances early on while in Iraq, when a vehicle he had owned was repossessed two years before, and the creditor decided to go after Chris for the balance even after reselling the vehicle.

This vehicle had been purchased by he and his wife in 2001 for the ready-made family he married into. Unfortunately, she was not able to be on the title due to bad credit, so Chris was the sole responsible party all these years later.

Chris's first two months' worth of paychecks then went to that vehicle settlement. It was vitally important for him to take the settlement offered because his position in Iraq could've been compromised if he didn't. He didn't see a dime of earnings during that time just to settle the case! My heart ached for him. He just couldn't seem to get on top of things but didn't lose his spirit throughout the ordeal and got the matter successfully settled and off his record.

I had just returned from Montana when Chris asked me to look at the possibility of his purchasing a vehicle from Ford in Sioux Falls. So, I began to work with the salesman who has always helped us since we moved back to South Dakota. Chris's credit had taken such a hit with all the bills dumped on him from the divorce and long-term separation. He had bills on his credit report that he didn't even

  Linda J. Johnson

know were assigned to him, including medical co-pays and deductibles for his kids. It would take a lot of time and effort to dispute those in the days ahead, in order to get Chris approved for a truck.

Chris was approved for a lease, and later on he could decide to purchase this vehicle if he so desired. Chris chose a vehicle on the lot, and our friend and salesman for Ford planned to drive it down to Kansas City for Chris to pick up when he got in on leave. Chris has been so proud of that truck.

During the month before Chris arrived, he phoned to tell me that HR personnel had called him in for a questionable e-mail he had forwarded. I had forwarded this same e-mail to him a few months before that time and didn't even remember it. The e-mail, which was entitled "Why is it that only whites can be racist?" was just one that I had actually received from Iraq in the first place. I looked for it on my computer and brought it up to print and reviewed it. This opinion e-mail had circulated both inside the military and in the U.S. It speaks to the frustration of Caucasians being confronted with racism and bigotry because of their skin color, or maybe I should say lack of color! Anyway, Chris had forwarded it to a few people on his personal e-mail and on his personal downtime.

Chris had then forwarded it to another employee, and that employee had e-mailed it on. So, the person who claimed offense didn't even receive it from Chris but made a complaint to HR. Chris was held accountable for this. He actually then apologized to anyone who might have been offended and explained that it was just a forward and not authored by him. He meant nothing by it. It went downhill from there without Chris even knowing about it. The personnel representative for the site accepted Chris's explanation.

Chris did not receive a write-up for the incident, as company policy states, if further action would be deemed necessary. The head of personnel for that site was transferred to another base at this same time, along with quite a few people who jumped ship with the management change. His dad and I told him, "Don't worry about this. It wasn't authored by you. It was an opinion e-mail and not personally meant for anyone in particular."

The statement I am going to make is my opinion on the use of, or interpretation of, affirmative action policies that U.S. companies have adopted. It would appear that more often than not, the rules in place now actually can cause discrimination against Caucasian employees, and most often male Caucasian employees. It doesn't appear to be fair that the tables can be turned and a group of male employees can be made to feel uncomfortable or sense that they are walking on eggshells simply because this policy includes deference for race and gender, but excludes them.

Chris proceeded to train someone to take his place while he would be gone on leave. He was eagerly looking forward to seeing his kids again and moving forward with his life. At the same time though, he had gotten a "Dear John" letter from a gal he had become very interested in. So, Chris was having a rough time.

I told him that even though he was planning on bringing the kids up here the second week of September, I would come down and attend the circus with him on September 8, 2007, ahead of his visit here. He had purchased reserved seats and

  Linda J. Johnson

was excited about his kids' anticipation of the event. I asked my sister to attend with us, and she was looking forward to it. We would become his "dates" for the evening, along with his kids!

This was Chris treating us all to a night out! I spent the night of the event at my sister's home in Kansas City, and the kids were ecstatic that night. I was so happy to see Chris being the provider, father, and son he knew he could be. He was maturing before my eyes.

I reflected on what a wonderful time we had at the circus and in Kansas City on such a short trip for me. The next day I drove home toward South Dakota. I was at peace. Chris was doing well, and the kids seemed happy to see me, their daddy, and their aunt. Chris had his self-esteem restored, and he felt he was contributing to the effort in Iraq. He was on the road to recovering from the emotional turmoil he had been in for the past few years.

I got going that afternoon with a light heart and very happy for Chris. Then I got a call from him while I was driving home. He was frantic!

Someone from personnel for the corporation, from Fayetteville, Georgia, called him that day and told him that the company wasn't renewing his contract. Later he found out he was actually terminated. The woman told Chris it was due to an e-mail incident. Chris was so shocked that he didn't even know what to say. She told him a letter would be coming to him and that he should sign it. I told him, "Don't sign anything."

What a nightmare! Chris was now faced with a leased vehicle payment of $407/monthly, over $650/monthly in child support payments, and actually no permanent place to live. He had no plans for an immediate future back in the States because he was going back to Iraq. All of his personal possessions stateside were in storage. Now what would he do?

I contacted the Deputy Program Manager in Iraq. This was the same man who had befriended our family early on. He sent an e-mail back telling Rich and me that he would look into the incident and get back to us. We are still waiting! Chris has left numerous phone messages for this man and has received no feedback. Chris has never had a chance to explain what may have happened, nor did he now know what to do.[1]

All of Chris's belongings were still in Iraq (TV, camera, pictures of family, clothing). He had purchased the airline ticket to get home and back to Iraq expecting the reimbursement, which is fully reimbursed to the men on leaves numbered three, six, and nine, and now he didn't know if he would have that reimbursement coming back to him!

Chris was totally devastated, embarrassed, and completely distressed. He could never really tell people what had happened because he doesn't understand it to this day.

As he tells it, the site manager came to him before he had left on his leave and told him, "Just go home and don't worry about anything here. It will all be taken care of until you get back." Then, apparently, another action was taken against Chris, without his ever being given the chance to defend himself.

The company had also terminated the guy who had actually forwarded the purportedly offensive e-mail to others. This action ended a long-term career for that man, who had been in Iraq for a long time.

Chris was so shocked over this. He had never been given a warning or infraction on the job. In fact, in the course of a

  Linda J. Johnson

few months, he was promoted twice. He was also being eyed for the next level position in Iraq by the gal who first recommended him. Chris did talk with a few employees who were still in Iraq, and they were also shocked by the action. They told him if anything the incident should've warranted a suspension day without pay, maybe, but this overreaction? Never!

This action was inconceivable to me on the part of the company. I spoke to Rich, and he was powerless to do anything. He was in Iraq and couldn't jeopardize his own position. Besides, he was stationed at a completely different base and site. He wasn't a party to the incident and couldn't imagine what was going on. He couldn't jump into the middle of this because he didn't know what had happened. We have heard that many, many employees left that site in the next few months.

Chris asked for a hearing from personnel and was flatly ignored. He didn't sign the letter they sent nor send it back to them. He waited a total of three months before a few of the crates arrived with his belongings, and at the end of March 2008, he received the last of the items. He was still missing his camera and awards, including gold coins awarded to him for excellent work performed in Iraq. All the items from his office have never been sent to date.

Like Chris says, he had no place to turn, no protection for his job, and no hearing or consideration given to him to dispute the accusations that apparently got him terminated. He simply had no recourse. One man had sealed Chris's fate. This action by the company affected not only Chris personally but his kids and their livelihood, along with all of their insurance coverage. It adversely affected all of us.

My husband had to send $250 in cash up to the site manager in order for them to send Chris's belongings home. They didn't send them home on their dime, and they didn't reimburse his airline ticket. Chris was expecting this reimbursement to help tide him over.

Chris filed for and went on unemployment immediately, waiting for the company to respond. I always believed he would be restored to his position once the company heard the entire story of his termination. It wasn't to be. They completely and utterly ignored him. The disconnect between the company in Iraq and the company stateside is sometimes uncanny. The victims of this disconnect are our family members.

There was a hearing that came up to dispute Chris's unemployment received in the state of Kansas, but the company did not participate in the phone conference with the judge, so Chris won. The company had cited policies from an employee handbook, or policy manual, which neither Chris nor Rich had ever received nor seen. This was used in the paperwork they sent to the unemployment division at the end of the year. This was the first time Chris actually got to see what their case would be. He had never received any of that information when he asked for it, week after week.

We had sent in the papers for him explaining everything that had happened, and I believe this helped him. The positive end to this is that Chris made the most of an unfortunate incident and felt that he could at least be there now for his kids. He has started a good position with Citibank and is getting on with his life.

I have heard about stories like this coming out of Iraq, and not just from my husband's company. Other companies have been notorious for dumping men at whim inside Iraq.

  Linda J. Johnson

Iraq is another world, and they don't play by rules that would protect American citizens employed by American companies. If this were to have happened stateside, Chris would have had more recourse. I was grieving in my heart for my son. Our extended family and friends were also in disbelief. It would appear that no one could or would advise Chris on what to do because it was already done.

In addition to all of this, Chris has suffered recurring attacks of nightmares and anxiety attacks at night. They are becoming more frequent and affect his ability to cope. He has had incidents during the day while driving. I believe that all of this is due to his negative experiences in a war zone and in Iraq. I worry for him and his well-being in the days ahead.

I did speak to an attorney who specializes in "whistle blower" cases from Chicago. He was very kind and considerate. We discussed what had happened. He read the e-mail that Chris had sent and said, "It is possible that the company could or would do this based on that e-mail." He also said it is possible that Chris was a victim of discrimination based on race or gender, but he wouldn't be able to prove this without Chris having some of his own files.

Actually, Chris was only interested in being restored to his position. We wrote to corporate and to company headquarters, or the parent company. We received no calls, letters, or approach from them to talk to Chris. It was unbelievable to me. They just shut down on Chris.

Chris never got to go back to Iraq, so he was powerless to discuss any of the company's actions. All of his files were there inside Iraq. The attorney told me that if Chris wanted to discuss any company indiscretions in regards to company actions that Chris had observed, or if Chris had anything to divulge regarding the company doing business in a manner that could be construed as unsavory, then he could consider taking the case. Chris said, "What can I say? I have nothing here; all of my files are in Iraq."

When Chris brought his kids up for September 13–16, we both still believed that someone from the company would call him. We thought either the Iraq Program Management Office or someone from stateside personnel would get involved. It didn't happen. Not even a courtesy call from HR.

I couldn't believe the calloused treatment of American contractors that I had heard about until it happened within our family. Chris suffered this silently and alone. He didn't want to discuss it within the family or extended family. He had been so proud of his contribution and work there and had decided to make a career with the company post-Iraq.

Chris has been affected permanently by this negative experience. We are powerless to help him. We know Chris would like to go back to Iraq, but he hasn't been given the chance. He doesn't want to talk to another company that is recruiting for Iraq yet. My concern for Chris over this, combined with the worry for Rich, is almost too much to bear on some days.

  Linda J. Johnson

CHAPTER 36

I often wonder now what will happen when large numbers of contractors come home to the States. Rich tells me that they talk about it all the time there on base. There are no jobs for them stateside. They are exactly like OCWs, overseas contract workers that leave third-world countries to work in another country to support their families.

That concept has been going on for years among people in poor countries. Now it is going on in America. Again, many of these guys are from military families or are vets themselves, but not career military. So, if the unemployment figures seem high now, I wonder what will happen when we leave the Middle East.

State by state, families and lives will be impacted by those men coming home when they are thrown into the job market and find no jobs will be available for them. They are too old to enlist or re-enlist.

I've seen the impact this has on families already by what happened when Kauai National Guard returned. Some didn't go back to their previous civilian jobs, and none of them earned what they had earned while deployed. In fact, the disparity in their pay was like a windfall to them while they were deployed. They were never able to match those earnings back in Hawaii. Some had even received combat-related injuries and went on medical benefits or disability from the national guard to offset the loss of income.

No one probably knows how many people, besides the military, will be affected long term by combat/stress-related trauma. Families have been negatively affected as well by the separations. Many have sought personal marriage counseling during and after their tours.

We read about all of the steps being taken by the military to help our troops during re-entry; however, who is going to be there for us? Our families will not have Post Traumatic Stress Disorder counseling available or a V.A. hospital to go to. We won't even have consistent health insurance or benefits that would continue. It is frightening. The price we pay to send a loved one into this conflict is not measurable yet.

Our men will have to re-enter normal life in the States, if you will, on their own. They won't be together in the same state as a team to be able to call upon one another. Rich and I even talk about whether he will get to visit or see the guys he has spent so much time with when he gets back to the States.

They have been through experiences that I cannot even imagine. They have only had each other in a loose-structure-type way. Rich tells me that is why he is careful not to make too many close associations, because things change there and nothing is for sure. I know it is hard on him. There were only two other guys who were on the base who had been there with him this entire time. They were the long-term guys—one has transferred to another company, and James (name changed) went home.

I have read various articles in the *USA Today* newspaper about a study being done to evaluate possible negative effects on American diplomats stationed in a war zone. The question crossed my mind as to where are the studies that should be done for people like Rich, who has now done a prolonged stint in a war zone since August of 2005?

Some of the contractors with the company have been in Iraq much longer than Rich. What about them? Who is looking out for our American military contractors? They have a voice and have lived there in as much trauma as anyone else stationed in a war zone. Rich has stayed at D-2, right in the middle of the action, for his entire deployment. Although he doesn't leave the Green Zone, he is affected. However, the study was being done on those diplomats stationed at the embassy down the street from where he has been! Those diplomats are stationed in the Green Zone as well. Our men have seen and experienced things just like the diplomats and many of the troops, but no one is talking about them much.

During the latter part of 2007, I noticed that security contractors from Blackwater Worldwide were all over the media. These guys, of whom many are armed contractors and work outside the wire, are very important to our mission in Iraq. The bad press they received made me heartsick for a lot of reasons. They were accused of unnecessary firing into a group of Iraqi civilians, causing death of innocents. I don't know the story, but I wonder at the constant reporting, investigating, and the portrayal of these men as the "bad guys."

Recently, Blackwater's contract was renewed for one more year inside Iraq. Once again bad press stories came out showing Iraqis protesting this action. I doubt that the protest would've been widespread among Iraqis, except that our press keeps "dogging" Blackwater stirring up the hatred or distrust against them. I believe my husband when he tells me that the press is only allowed in certain areas inside Iraq, so it would be near to impossible for them to fairly report both sides of an issue they want to report back to the American people. If they want to "demonize" a company, Blackwater seems to be their target of choice!

In a rare appearance to defend security contractors and in an article published last May, Erik Prince, the founder of Blackwater, was featured. I want to cite some of what he said regarding the accusations against them of being "mercenaries" on some kind of aggressive mission to kill or maim anyone: "Blackwater Founder Eric Prince defends defense contractors: by Ted Roelofs, The Grand Rapids Pres" (partial article).

> Grand Rapids…To Blackwater Worldwide founder Erik Prince, the use of private security firms in a troubled world makes perfect sense…"They have been there all through history," Prince said, citing privateers from John Paul Jones to Thaddeus Kosciuszko, head engineer of the Continental Army…Blackwater has been praised by advocates for doing a difficult job under tough circumstances

  Linda J. Johnson

and condemned by critics for mercenary values and sloppy oversight... It came under intense scrutiny in September 2007 after Blackwater guards killed 17 Iraqi civilians in a Baghdad shooting incident that remains under investigation. Preliminary reports indicate the guards were not fired upon... Prince did not mention the September incident. He said Blackwater has carried out about 19,000 missions without losing a client... He said less than one-half of 1 percent of those (missions) involved the discharge of firearms by a Blackwater security guard... [1]

Interestingly, in an *Army Times* article on 7–21–08, Erik Prince was interviewed again, and he was asked about the September 2007 incident involving deaths of Iraqis and other allegations against him.

"We can take those lumps" When asked what constrains him when it comes to publicly explaining the allegations against him, he replies that for working in Iraq for the State Department, the contract says he will have no contact with the media, and hence he cannot put the facts out whenever he is attacked. He says that there is so much to renegotiate with the Department if his own employees are prosecuted under the Iraqi law. Prince adds here that Blackwater works for other countries too, like Azerbaijan. [2]

In researching this company, I came across an additional article in the *Air Force Times* entitled "Blackwater May protect shipping firms." An abstract of the article reads,

> "Blackwater Worldwide and 13 shipping firms are interested in hiring the McArthur Ship to accompany their cargo vessels through the coasts off the horn of Africa which are plagued with pirates, according to Blackwater chief executive CEO Erik Prince. He cited that the company's ships, its aircraft and boats will conduct a maritime version of personal security. He also stated that the crew of the ship will set clear policies on the use of force against pirates." [3]

I would venture to say that this is a good thing and could benefit many countries who have become the victims of these high seas marauders. I cannot understand why we don't stand up and support Americans who will go to the aid of other countries like this. This company is providing jobs for Americans at a time when jobs are becoming harder to come by! In my humble opinion, they have also stayed true to their mission. My husband's best friend inside Iraq has gone to work for them and I know Rich would go with them as a mechanic, in a heartbeat, if the opportunity came along.

Rich says many guys would like to get on with Blackwater. He relates that they take care of their own guys and stick together like brothers. He also says they pay at one of the best rates in the industry, and anyone who gets on with them knows in advance exactly what he or she is supposed to do within their company. The men of Blackwater know what they are getting into when they are hired, and despite being called everything from "escapees from the rat race ... to the perpetually bored," they are hired to do a job.

I wonder, as I read the articles from the press and view the vicious nature of online pundits attacking this guy, if

  Linda J. Johnson

the attacks on Blackwater aren't related to the fact that Erik Prince has never hidden the fact that he is a committed conservative Christian and has been a Republican supporter of George W. Bush?

To me, it appears that he has come under the same kind of scrutiny and criticism that many other high profile Christians have come under in most recent years by the liberal mainstream media.

Why is the media continuously bashing and harassing Americans who are Christians and patriots, and yet they ignore the more obvious target of those who are the enemy of America? Why are security contractors' guard jobs of so much interest to the press? Why is the press using manipulation to sway public opinion against these Americans?

Recently, in the *Army Times*, November 24, 2008, a new book was reviewed, *Big Boy Rules*. I believe that this book will be an important read for those who want to understand American security guards and their families.[4]

These people are definitely a group that has gotten much more negative press than my husband and the military contractors working on bases, but I don't believe it makes them any less American or the reasons for their going any less valid.

Why isn't there more attention paid to people like Muslims of charity groups located inside America who are funding terrorist groups committed to killing Americans and Christians, Jews or non-Muslims?

The *USA Today* ran a small national news item, "Charity leaders convicted of aiding Hamas" on November 25, 2008. The article discussed the fact that five leaders of the Holy Land Foundation, once the nation's largest Muslim charity, were convicted Monday, November 24, 2008, in Dallas of sending more than $12 million to Hamas-run schools, hospitals, and social welfare programs in Palestinian territories. 108 charges were brought, including money laundering, conspiracy, supporting a terrorist group, and tax fraud.[5]

Where are the books and articles regarding these activities? Where is the outrage that should be expressed by TV talk show hosts and mainstream media news programs over these stories? What are we doing bashing one another and wasting time letting a potentially dangerous problem arise within our own borders? What is our Congress doing fighting amongst themselves and discussing how much money might be "wasted" inside Iraq, and yet they would fail to see the danger for Americans upon our own land? Who is the real enemy here?

Lest we forget the mission of Hamas, let's revisit what they stand for in a part of their charter statement:

> "This is the Charter of the Islamic Resistance..."
>
> Hamas which will reveal its face, unveil its identity, state its position, clarify its purpose, discuss its hopes, call for support to its cause and reinforcement, and for joining its ranks. For our struggle against the Jews is extremely wide-ranging and grave, so much so that it will need all the loyal efforts we can wield, to be followed by further steps and reinforced by successive battalions from the multifarious Arab and Islamic world, until the enemies are defeated and Allah's victory prevails. Thus we shall perceive them approaching in the horizon, and this will be known before long... As the Movement adopts Islam as its way of life, its time dimension extends back as far as the birth of

Linda J. Johnson

the Islamic Message and of the Righteous Ancestor. Its ultimate goal is Islam, the Prophet its model, the Quran its Constitution. Its spacial dimension extends wherever on earth there are Muslims, who adopt Islam as their way of life; thus, it penetrates to the deepest reaches of the land and to the highest spheres of Heavens. THE CHARTER OF ALLAH: THE PLATFORM OF THE ISLAMIC RESISTANCE MOVEMENT (HAMAS)[6]

Yet so often we are told to be politically correct in this country and go ahead and bash the Iraq war and President George W. Bush, yet tolerate those living among us who do not share our founding fathers' ideology, and in fact hope for the demise or change of America to a nation that would persecute someone like me for my beliefs. For me, we are demonizing the wrong people and forgetting what our mission has been on behalf of the war on terror! We are making the wrong people the enemy and making our enemies the victims!

Rich just has a fit when he hears what is happening here inside America since he has been deployed. He keeps telling me that what he hears about the change of tide in Americans' unity and opinion cannot be happening. I tell him, "It definitely has changed since you left. This is not the same America you all thought you would come home to."

He asks me if everyone is oblivious to what would happen if Americans don't connect the dots back to Iraq. I tell him that they aren't. I tell him unfortunately a big issue for Americans is to bring everyone home from Iraq and demonize the contracting corporations or companies but ignore the obvious.

The constant negative rhetoric regarding contractors in

general is very hard on me. I take it personally every time someone attacks our Americans working over there. This burden to set the record straight has been on my mind since the beginning of Rich's deployment.

I've had so many conversations about contractors in Iraq. So many Americans don't know us. They don't know who we are or why our families are there. Mostly they are caught up in change rhetoric and anti-Iraq and anti-Bush rhetoric. It gives me an uneasy feeling within my being to watch it happening. The lack of understanding as to how our men are interdependent upon the military is sadly widespread.

Like Rich will always tell me, "[The army] always comes around to working with us. They begin to appreciate us when they realize our role and how we help each other out." Due to bad press from the American media, many troops or detachments that arrive in Iraq can be unfriendly or difficult for our company technicians at first.

The army's division stationed where Rich is assigned has now changed for the third time since Rich has been in. They are all stationed at Camp Prosperity, and Rich says these new guys weren't friendly at first. He tells me, "Don't worry; they will be." He has been in there this long, and he knows now how it will go. It just may take longer for the cooperation to come.

Eventually these guys who have just started rotation in there will be working side by side with my husband and his unit. They will understand how very important they all are to each other. They will get it. They will appreciate the cooperation and understand it is very important to the success of the overall mission in Iraq, especially there in Baghdad during a time of transition.

  Linda J. Johnson

CHAPTER 37

Oftentimes, I feel helpless as I wonder how I can lift up the guys and convey to them a little reminder that people are thinking about them and send in some little piece of America to them. October was no different than the year before, as I thought that they needed a pick me up before the holiday season would approach when they would begin to receive more mail again.

These were just some Halloween treat bags for fun for them to enjoy. I spent a day and half shopping, sorting, and packing those for the guys. This is something I can do to help support them at a time when not much is being sent in for them. It was earlier than the holiday season, and mostly it was just a reminder that someone is thinking about them and appreciating them. I always hope that the efforts will be something fun to take their minds off of where they are.

Also in October, one of the ladies' groups at the Methodist church I had been attending confirmed that they would indeed sponsor our guys for Christmas. I was so relieved. At that time, Rich had been in Iraq for three Christmas holidays, and to date one group or another had stepped up to sponsor them to help make their holiday season merrier.

The Christmas of 2007 would be no exception. These ladies really outdid themselves with blessings extended to these men.

This church had also been publishing Rich's name weekly in their bulletin as a reminder to pray for him and the men. This was very comforting to me.

The ladies baked over forty-dozen homemade goodies for our guys. Also, they started a church-wide drive to gather each man a new bath towel, individual hygiene products, goodies, magazines, batteries, coffee, and microwaveable foods (just to name a few of the items).

They included two very special items in their gift to the men: a New Testament camouflage Bible and a homemade, patriotic pillowcase. The men were thrilled, according to Rich, when they received them and put their pillowcases on the bunks immediately! It was such a personal and uplifting touch to the gift boxes.

The church spent over $700 on postage to get the priority mail boxes in there. The entire church helped out with the project. Each individual group within this church gave funds to see the project turn out a success! It was very humbling.

Rich would be in on leave right at the time the project was due to ship, and he was able meet a few of the ladies and gave them thanks personally for what they would do for his unit.

  Linda J. Johnson

Rich's sixth leave began in November. He arrived in Sioux Falls in almost balmy weather for mid-November. We had decided to host his family for Thanksgiving. I was so busy ahead of his arrival getting everything we would need to host so many people. This had been our biggest gathering yet in the house.

Chris brought up his two kids for this holiday. We were all excited to have our first holiday get-together since 2003. Rich hadn't seen Chris since March, when Chris had transferred up to Al Asad Air Base. They had lots to talk about with what had happened to Chris.

I noticed how tired Rich was. I think he slept more than ever the first three days of this leave. I had a small project list for him, and he got involved into the routine of being home rather quickly. He always tells me that I also seem to relax and rest better when he is here.

As for me, of course, I would relax. My better half is home and by my side! That in itself has a very calming effect on me. We've both said that this stint of being married and living so far apart is not the norm, and we don't recommend it for everyone.

When he does finally come home, however, it will be easier for us to accept any type of work schedule. At least he would be in-country! After all, we've done this the hard way now. We've had oceans and continents between us.

It appears that in the future we will be really flexible in accepting whatever schedules or demands any job would entail. The fact that Rich can be so flexible in such a demanding and chaotic work environment in the midst of a war zone makes me so proud of him. He can roll with the flow and adapts there daily. I am amazed at his ability to do this!

It was wonderful to host his family at Thanksgiving in our home. We cooked a twenty-eight-pound turkey and a sixteen-pound ham. There was plenty of food and fun for all. Even the weather cooperated.

We both remembered this same weekend thirty years before. We had gotten married on Thanksgiving Saturday in 1977. A blizzard blew in on that Saturday evening, and we never got out of town. But this Thanksgiving was wonderful weather in comparison.

Chris and his kids left the day after Thanksgiving, and Jada cried because she was saying good-bye to her grandpa. Jada always seems to know that whenever she tells her grandpa good-bye it may be months or even years before she sees him again. It breaks her heart and ours. She told him, "Grandpa, just be there for my next birthday." He smiled, and it just might've happened, but Chris wasn't able to bring his children up for Rich's March 2008 leave. Jada turned seven years old on March 22, 2008. Rich and I didn't get to see her or her brother until July of 2008.

My sister Cathy and her husband, Mark, from Rapid City, South Dakota, came for a short visit after Thanksgiving. It was very, very cold out. We had a nice time despite the cold that had settled in. She hadn't seen Rich since 2004, before we left for Kauai. So, we spent a nice couple of days visiting with them.

The one thing we both appreciated for that leave was that it was so relaxing, and we got to stay mostly at home. This is what Rich likes the most—just being home in his house. It appeared it would be harder than ever to let him go

  Linda J. Johnson

back. I didn't have any big plans on the horizon. The winter would prove to be long and cold.

Rich had seen the temperatures fluctuate by thirty to forty degrees during that leave. He thought that at least when he went back into the Middle East it would be warmer than South Dakota. Although it was the rainy season there in Iraq, the next six months would prove to be colder and damper than usual in his opinion. Many of them would get sick.

Right before this leave the men were subjected to a surprise inspection of quarters. This latest inspection occurred in the middle of the night, right before Rich was to come home. He was awakened at 1:30 a.m., and his living quarters were inspected. As a result of this inspection, six men and the site manager left the company.

Once again, the master mechanic and foreman position for the base opened up. I encouraged him to apply because he was so down about his last rejection letter. After all, he had filled in for the foreman regularly, and he was already a senior mechanic when he went into Iraq. Rich is a trained brake and alignment specialist and is recognized as such. He also regularly filled in for the QAQC on base.

Rich got notification that he would be interviewed for the master mechanic job while he was home on leave. Again we both laughed because we knew it would be a conference call in the middle of the night. This was a $3/hour raise or so and very important to Rich. After all, he had already received his two-year consecutive appreciation award for work in Iraq from the company and from all four branches of the military. It was really his time to earn what he was worth and already performing.

Because the wheel mechanics were getting no raises in

wages or increases in their airfare reimbursement for leave, we were actually seeing our budget erode each year that he had been in there, especially during the times that he took leaves.

Rich's original recruiter called from Iraq about an hour ahead of his interview to give him a heads up and remind him of the schedule. He was excited and hopeful once again. This time, after a very good interview, he was successful. The base e-mailed him with his paperwork to sign, and he got some congratulations in e-mails from the guys. We were so very thankful for this promotion. Rich had earned it, and he deserved it.

After all the hard work; the consistent, steady employment; and the fact that he had received no safety violations and no negative write-ups, Rich had finally been given his due. Up to that point, Rich had also never had a sick day.

The most important thing about this promotion was that Rich didn't want to leave his site. He wanted a promotion on his own site, and he got it! I have always felt that Rich has favor. I know through our faith that God has his hand upon my husband. All things happen for a reason.

It was bittersweet when Chris came home at Thanksgiving and had to congratulate his dad. Chris was still hurting from his experience with the company, but he knew his dad earned this. I wanted to cry. Chris longed to go back with the company to Iraq to clear his name and set the record straight. Rich couldn't do anything for him. Chris wanted a chance to be heard and fairly judged for his hard work and performance there. It was a dilemma for our family.

Rich e-mailed the HR rep, who had been his original recruiter, and thanked him for the "nod" for his promotion. They had truly come a long way since Houston and August of 2005.

  Linda J. Johnson

We made the announcement to his family at Thanksgiving. They were very happy, but one of his sisters said to me, "This must mean he'll stay there longer."

I told her, "Yes, I think so," with a sigh.

CHAPTER 38

December 6 came fast and then he was gone! I did some more substitute teaching and volunteered for some shifts at the community's angel-tree project through the Salvation Army. This gave me something to focus on to get through the holidays. I even worked on Christmas Eve. Then I went on to Rich's family in Pipestone, Minnesota, for their annual gathering. I wanted to just be home in South Dakota and not travel very far. If Rich could do it alone, then I could do it alone. Anyway, we had already had our Christmas in November while he was home.

I also joined a Bible study group at the local Salvation Army, which had given me a few close female friends to share with without compromising Rich and his position in any way. They have been a very helpful group to me and understand what I am going through.

When Rich went back to Iraq, he was battling sinus and cold problems. For the first time in his deployment, he had to see the medic. He was given Sudafed and didn't miss any work, but he kept battling the same cold and flu-like symptoms for the next few months.

He had gotten his flu shot at home, so we didn't really think he would be susceptible to any flu issues. However, the winter of 2007–2008, or rainy season over in Iraq, was proving to be cold and wet, and his body was run down.

The first sick day that Rich has ever had was in Iraq early this year. He had gone over two years without taking a sick day and had accumulated sick leave hours. It appears that he won't arbitrarily use them or be paid for them even though his performance has been exemplary while deployed! When I ask him why, he tells me, "They don't want us to get sick. It could be an indication of your ability to do the job, and it is such a hassle because we have to go to the medic and get a sick slip and present it on-site before we go back to bed to be sick!"

We receive Department of Defense forms whenever he sees the medic, and these read something about our men being injured or having come down with an illness while on the job or in Iraq. They then get their benefits, but not unless they are on the job.

Well, to me that is absurd. They are on the job every day and live on the job. They are even on the job while they are home because they have to go back or face loss of all benefits and immediate termination. For us, while he is home, we are also online with the base and some of the men, and there is always something to send back in to Iraq. They are on ten days' pay for leave, and the rest are LWOP (leave without

  Linda J. Johnson

pay) days of up to six additional. This pay is considerably less than what they earn in Iraq, so each leave is also a budget adjustment. We get hit with the airline ticket ahead of time and don't get reimbursed until they go back. This sick leave benefit is costly yet vitally necessary for their overall health and ability to perform in Iraq for a long period of time.

In January, he asked for a vaporizer/steamer. So, I purchased one and sent it to him in another care package. Along with it I packed candies and goodies for him. I can never seem to send in enough for his supply!

At the beginning of 2008, we also started feeling more comfortable and secure with where he was. It appeared to us that Baghdad had calmed down, and Rich and his men saw signs of that. For them there were fewer sirens and bombings, and chaos was infrequent. It became more novelty than the norm.

Meanwhile, I was preparing for a week in Arizona. I was going to visit our adult Filipino godchildren and their family. Also, I would spend a few days at the home of a very good friend and her husband who winter down there.

At the home of Richie Quillopo in Wickenburg, Arizona, we celebrated four January birthdays between us. It was a wonderful three days with them, and the weather was a godsend compared to South Dakota!

I hadn't seen their family for over two years and wanted to get back in touch. My mare' Lita, or Leah's mother, was also living with them again. I got to spend a little time with her. In Filipino culture the relationship between me as the godmother to Richie and Leah and Leah's mother is a very special one, so she is my kumare,' or closer than a sister. It was a grand event because we are like family.

We had a lot of catching up to do. I didn't even get a chance to visit with Rich's relatives who were visiting a niece of Rich's not far away from Wickenburg. I promised them that next time Rich would be with me, and we would spend more time there and see everyone!

Each day that I can schedule something is a day that goes by with something to do until he comes home again. That is how we live. I get to feeling so bad that he can't enjoy some of these activities or trips with me. He misses and has missed so much of the interaction with friends and family now for three years.

There are a few people, though, like Charlotte, who have stuck with us since the beginning of Rich's deployment. She calls almost daily to check on me and writes Rich regularly. She has truly been a blessing to us both.

Then there are Linda and Steve Davidson, who are long-time family friends. They have been a tremendous support to us both, along with their entire family. In fact, being back in South Dakota has allowed us to rekindle our longtime friendship, and it has been rewarding for all of us at this stage in our lives.

From January 20–24, 2008, I had a great second half of my visit in Arizona at Queen Creek. I spent time with Steve and Linda Davidson. It was so relaxing and refreshing for me. They really get where I am coming from too. I could unwind at their place. They included me in a few meaningful social events while I was there with their interesting circle of friends and family. I really felt like I re-entered the real world again. I am forever grateful to this wonderful couple for their friendship and outreach to both Rich and me.

Sometimes it has just been nice to be away from the

  Linda J. Johnson

pressure of all the household chores and problems to solve here at home. These mini-visits have seemed to refresh and strengthen me for the next few weeks and months ahead. I can face each new struggle with renewed optimism after I have gotten away for a while.

CHAPTER 39

Two days after I got home from Arizona, I was talking to Rich, and all of a sudden he had to hang up. They had an air raid, or call to hard buildings or bunker. It had been such a long time since this had happened to us that I freaked out.

When he phoned me back within the hour, I found out that they didn't know what really happened. But I was still shaken. It had been a long time since we had to go through that tension. And most of the time, he doesn't know what has happened, or at least not all of the details anyway. They aren't fully privy to this information. They see more about it on news that is flashed in the DFAC (dining facility), on their cable stations infrequently, or over the Internet. Then they have to reassure us back home that it hasn't affected them where they are.

We are getting news clips here after the fact, and Rich will say, "They are only reporting what they choose to report."

During the presidential primary season of 2008, it became clear that Iraq would be the factor that would divide Americans like never before. It was as if the politicians were playing for the largest prize at a carnival. It was heartbreaking and gut-wrenching every time one of them bashed or trashed President Bush and his eight years in office. The jokes and blunders about a sitting commander-in-chief and the fact that we had Americans deployed didn't seem to compute to some of those who acted to divide the nation daily into pro and con.

Protesters now didn't seem bothered about drawing attention to themselves and seemed on a mission of revenge. Rich and I discussed that many of them had never been to Iraq and couldn't speak to the situation of progress, and they most certainly didn't understand the pride that Americans who had deployed there felt in the role they played. Many of the protestors had never been in the military, and didn't know how much their actions would affect the families back home.

We know that it is not even feasibly possible to evacuate or withdraw our people from Iraq in a short amount of time. According to the "Report of the Task Force for a Responsible Withdrawal from Iraq," our troops couldn't even get out of Iraq unless we worked it out logistically for a period of between twelve to eighteen months! We also believe in our mission there, anyway.[1]

We really believe our mission must and will succeed. The U.S.A. needs to help stabilize the Middle East and help Iraq rise again as a democracy. This is most important to us as

  Linda J. Johnson

a nation since September 11, 2001. The Islamic world will view any move we make in the future with Iraq in terms of strength or weakness. If we remain committed to seeing Iraq succeed, we will earn some respect of those who would continue to wish us harm. If we retreat too early and Iraq fails, or something untoward happens to them from other nearby invading nations, America will be blamed.

One day they will all come home, but for now they work together as comrades on one of the most important missions facing Americans in the world today. One day Americans will understand the important and unique role that each and every person who has deployed to Iraq or Afghanistan, has played.

My prayer is that men like my husband will continue to hold their heads up and stand proud of the service they have contributed for our country's freedom and stability. Maybe more people will thank them as they understand the unique sacrifices the contractors have made.

During the first two months of 2008, we went through more complications. Rich called one day on his regular, longer call and told me that they were almost out of coffee in the PX. He said he didn't know why the PX wasn't stocking many goods, but at this rate, they wouldn't have any coffee, creamers, or sugar. I told him, "Don't worry; we'll get you in some coffee." Within a week, my Tuesday study group had packed two large boxes for the men.

We had four large coffee canisters, creamers, and sugars sent in, along with goodies that the gals purchased for all of them. We also packed candies of all varieties and beef jerky. You name it; we packed those boxes full. It was lots of fun to get these care packages ready once again for the men.

I mailed them off, and they arrived to an outburst of glee from the guys, within seven days. The guys e-mailed back to us a couple of photos of the men receiving the boxes. Rich said the coffee came just in time. They were so very happy, and so were we!

Then, within a day after receiving those boxes and distributing everything, Rich got even sicker. He had to go see the medic again. This time, he missed half a day at work. This would be the first sick leave time, or sick pay, that he had ever had on the job.

Within forty-eight hours of completing his fourth move to different living quarters, he came down really ill. I got an e-mail from the administrator (his roommate) telling me that Rich wasn't sleeping at night and that he was really, really sick. By the time I reached him, he had gone back to the medic and had gotten a shot for nausea, along with an antibiotic. He had been ordered to his bed! I was so scared for him. This just wasn't like Rich. He couldn't seem to shake this bug.

I phoned his Anthem insurance line, and a nurse got on the phone with Rich and me after I had given her his private cell phone number. She basically told him that if this treatment didn't stop the nausea or if the headache or vomiting returned, he should seek higher medical treatment.

Rich had told me that the medic inside Baghdad told him that if he didn't keep fluids down, he would send him to the Baghdad hospital for a drip. Rich vehemently opposed this plan. He had seen third-world hospitals before, and he frankly didn't want to come in contact with something worse than what he was suffering. When he told me, "I don't think I can take this anymore," meaning the way he felt so sick, I franti-

  Linda J. Johnson

cally got online and e-mailed or called in some prayer partners. I was really, really scared for Rich. Nobody had given him a diagnosis, so we didn't know what was wrong with him.

Within a few days, he was over everything except for losing his stomach contents. I sent him another antibiotic to take ahead of the trip home for his seventh R and R. He would be coming back to Sioux Falls in mid-March instead of late April. His request had been turned down because there were too many men now on the leave schedule. So, Rich was coming back home on leave earlier than he ever had in the past. I believed it couldn't be too soon so that he could rest and recover from whatever was wrong with him! The medic had mentioned the Iraqi flu, or "sand flea disease," and that freaked us both out. I was hoping he would be strong enough to make the flights home in March.

I want to speak about our health insurance for a moment. I noticed that back in 2007, something new was added to the leave request forms that Rich put in. If an employee visits a doctor or gets hospitalized, he is supposed to report it and get clearance to go back to Iraq from a company-chosen doctor.

To me this spelled trouble immediately. Why does someone who is paying for benefits like health insurance have to report health-related issues when they are home, on leave, in order to go back to Iraq? Furthermore, many of those guys are on maintenance meds and must have routine tests or preventative testing while they are home. These are benefits that take up our precious leave time in the first place and are our own personal business.

A buddy of Rich's got dental work with surgery done while home on leave and couldn't return to Iraq for a couple of months. The company had to clear him to return to his job. He was trying to get back to support his family, and they wouldn't allow it. Rich doesn't think he was paid during that time, but I do. Who knows?

  Linda J. Johnson

CHAPTER 40

Rich did get home in mid-March. I could tell he was dog-tired, but his flight in Atlanta had been cancelled ten minutes ahead of departure. He had to wait the entire day for connecting flights to Sioux Falls. This was after completing a fourteen-hour flight from Dubai. He didn't arrive in Sioux Falls until eight thirty on the evening of his scheduled arrival date.

In addition to the fact that he was so tired, it was cold here. We had a restful weekend and readjustment, but Rich started to feel like he was coming down with a cold once again! We had plans to go out to Rapid City, South Dakota, for a visit with my sister and her husband.

We loaded up on various over-the-counter cold meds for him and lots of vitamin C. I was sure that he was just travel sick, which has happened to both of us in the past.

We left Sioux Falls on a warmer, sunny day for a short

trip to Rapid City. This was the first road trip we had taken since the summer of 2005, before he left for Iraq. I was so excited to be having a normal getaway with my husband. Halfway into the drive, he told me he was nauseous again. I asked him if he wanted me to drive, to which he replied no.

When we arrived at my sister's house, Rich started feeling rough. That night he was back to vomiting and nausea and had signs of a very bad cold! So, we went to acute care to see a doctor. Rich got seen by an ex–air force doctor who was very kind and very thorough with him. He took blood work and made Rich give a stool sample to be checked for any possible intestinal parasites that Rich may have picked up in Iraq. We had the test results sent back to Sioux Falls in order for Rich to see his own doctor.

What a sad deal! I felt so sorry for my husband. He was so sick while we were visiting for the first time together at my sister's home. Despite all of this, we had a good reunion and headed back home the next day.

On Easter weekend, Rich and I had a quiet celebration. We had a Good Friday evening gathering at his sister's home in Pipestone, Minnesota. He finally ate a real meal. It was his first in three days. The meds that the doctor from Rapid City had given to him were working. We were so relieved.

On Monday, March 24, Rich saw his own doctor, and the doctor did some more tests and reported that Rich did not have any intestinal parasites. He didn't know what was causing the illness. In fact, Rich's doctor said he believed that Rich was just suffering a severe respiratory illness, with the other symptoms as byproducts. We were both relieved. His

  Linda J. Johnson

doctor took some more blood work and told Rich he would get back to him before Rich's scheduled flight on March 29.

Rich had a scan of his liver, pancreas, and gall bladder. They found nothing amiss, so Rich was good to go. He also had a dental exam, and his teeth cleaned that week.

This leave was the hardest on him. He was still recovering from being ill, and he didn't want to leave. Both of us were having a rough time with his departure.

We couldn't get any firm commitment from the base as to when he could put in next for a leave, and that distressed us. Because we live leave to leave, it would've been nice to put it on the calendar as a done deal. It is nice to have it on the schedule because then he has something to look forward to. Or, should I say, something to focus on day after difficult day inside Iraq.

His plane left on a dreary March Saturday afternoon. It did help that Delta had given me a gate pass to go with him up to the gates, because his plane left late. After that I really didn't have anywhere to turn. I knew that I couldn't just dump on anyone about how I felt. I did sense, though, that I was utterly and completely alone. I missed him this time more than ever, and I was worried about the long commute back to Iraq for him.

Once again, I would begin the long wait after his plane left Atlanta, until I heard from him at the BTC (Baghdad airport). He would then be able to tell me that he had arrived in Baghdad. While he was in Atlanta, we talked on the phone the entire time. Rich had broken his watch band at the Sioux Falls airport, so he had to purchase a new watch in Atlanta. He was asking me to look up the Atlanta field on the Internet and to find his concourse and tell him where he should look and what he should spend!

It was a very difficult six weeks following Rich's going back into Baghdad. I found myself plunging into the deepest depression that I had ever experienced this time around. It really didn't do me any good to attempt to explain it to anyone because no one else was going through exactly the same thing! I threw myself into activities.

  Linda J. Johnson

CHAPTER 41

Meanwhile, Chris was struggling at Kansas City, and we got an attorney for him to take on his case for the mediation and visitation along with the child support issues for his kids. He found himself experiencing night sweats and PTSD symptoms on a daily basis. My regular prayer group prayed around the clock for him, and within a few weeks he pulled himself together and began that new position at Citibank. God was working in ways I couldn't see to take the pressure off of me.

I was also working on this book and got quite a few sessions of writing in when I didn't take substitute teaching positions. All of this was going on, and the cloudy and cold weather seemed to never end. We had a spring season snowstorm on April 10, and Rich was shocked. I sent him some of the pictures, and he couldn't believe that we just couldn't shake the dreary weather here. He had fully recovered inside

Baghdad from the illness that plagued him while he was home. He knew that he wouldn't be able to get blood work done there and would have to wait to re-check his liver when he got back home next time.

We began the long wait until the end of July. All of the earlier June dates available for leave time were taken, and once again he would wait four long months to come home and then only get sixteen days when his contract year was almost up. In fact, when he was due to go back to Iraq, he was within two days of being eligible for a longer twenty-one-day leave. However, he was turned down when he asked if he could just skip leave eight and get paid for it and move on to leave nine in order to be home longer when he got here in the summer weather.

There had been so many news reports the weekend that he left of attacks directed against the Green Zone in Baghdad, so I was even more upset. It didn't help that I had a relative or two ask me if he would be safe in there. What was I to answer? I needed to hear from him in order to know what was really happening. I knew the media could be reporting this, and it might not be affecting them at all there. Like Rich has always told me, most of the action is down by the old U.S. Embassy and doesn't affect them as much where they are at.

One of his buddies e-mailed me that the latest incident occurred about a mile away and was not too serious. They heard some of the clatter, but it didn't directly cause them even to go to bunker. Thank God! Terry was always e-mailing me the same assuring message, "Nothing we can't handle."

Rich got back on base, and he was in short-sleeve T-shirts! I laughed as I told him that it had snowed twice since he left

  Linda J. Johnson

and that it was a very cold and rainy spring. In fact, our summer only began mid-June!

Once again I dealt with getting the lawn care set up and all the plants replaced that were eaten by rabbits! I have had great assistance from our landscaper, and he has been an invaluable help to me without Rich here. I kept snapping and sending in pictures to Rich of the progress. He recently told me he has a picture of the house right up on the computer so he can glance at it every day! It is another motivator for him.

Sometime during early summer, I read another article in the *USA Today* newspaper that talked about a defense contractor who was charged with gifting a certain congressman with gifts totaling over $700,000. It bothered me tremendously because I felt that the negative connotation would be directed towards all contractors. We subscribe to this newspaper in order that I can "take the posture" of America in its entirety.

Once again, I was sad to see that articles like this were taking precedence now about Iraq! It appeared to me that the focus was a "gotcha" mentality whenever some sordid account came up about fraud or corruption and the war. If I were to take the three years that my husband had worked inside Iraq and add up his take home earnings, he wouldn't even be close to being on track to earning $700,000 in *seven* years, yet alone see that much cash at one time inside Iraq. It is sad to read about these things.

It also saddened me to remember that during the year 2004 through the summer of 2006 while we were on Kauai, this same newspaper would publish daily, positive progress stories about Iraq, and I would clip them and read them inside our church services. Everyone liked to hear about something new beginning in Iraq because America had deployed there.

Again, the media appears to love to sensationalize a negative story these days about Iraq and doesn't appear to be too interested in the real stories of progress made by the presence of Americans inside Iraq.

I also read recently again about those security contractors who had gone missing over a year ago with Crescent Corporation. Their bodies had been found inside Iraq. Some of their severed fingers had been sent first to our military, and after that, the remains were found. These men were working for a Kuwait-based contracting company as armed security contractors.

I'm not sure what they earned in their respective positions, but I do know that there is a controversy surrounding their positions and what they were doing when they were kidnapped while escorting a convoy from Kuwait through Iraq. Regardless, it is sad, and my heart goes out to the families. It is just so much more dangerous than what my husband or son has ever done there. Their jobs are outside the wire. I am anxious to get a copy of the book that I have mentioned before, *Big Boy Rules*, which investigates what happened before, during, and after the November 16, 2006, kidnapping and took sixteen months to resolve.

Rich and I have settled into a routine now that works for us. I believe that we are adjusted and not just "used to" this life. He is phoning every other morning for his longer call. We talk as he needs to in between that schedule, or he e-mails and asks for one thing or another.

It's interesting when we both think we have told each

  Linda J. Johnson

other something that has happened to us, and as we are conversing, we realize we haven't! I don't know how much of our lives we are missing without being together. We will have to relearn and readjust when he finally comes home for good.

He finally received his itinerary for his summer 2008 leave. That was a special challenge again. The cost of airline tickets was escalating. The route he had become familiar with from Atlanta directly to Sioux Falls was cancelled by Delta. We had to get creative and bring him into Minneapolis. I then used his airline points to reserve another separate ticket to bring him home to Sioux Falls. This action saved us approximately $300.

Immediately after we got everything arranged for his summer leave, we began to discuss whether he could bring his carry-on and backpack together home on his next leave. He was concerned about it. They don't hassle him at Dubai when he boards the international flight. When he arrives in the U.S.A., however, he is given a hard time by the domestic airlines. Now he is limited as to the number of pounds in his gear leaving Iraq and then hassled within the U.S.A. just to get home. What little he has to carry home with him shouldn't be subject to any problems from the airlines in the first place!

CHAPTER 42

At the end of April, I decided to use our airline miles accumulated to book a short trip over to Ohio to visit our oldest son and his family. I hadn't seen them since early 2005 on Kauai, and it was a long overdue trip. I asked my mother to accompany me so that I would have a companion. We planned this for June, as close as possible to the fourth and sixth birthdays of our grandchildren, Jaclyn and Luke. This plan gave me something to look forward to again, and when the time came to go to Frank's, Rich's next leave would only be a short month away.

May brought two weddings and a funeral for our extended family. One of my aunts died in a relatively short time after being diagnosed with fast-spreading cancer. The weddings were for a cousin and nephew. These events reminded me that the cycle of life continues no matter where we are and what we are doing. People are born, they marry, and they live out their lives and die. It was an emotional time, as my cousin's daughter who was getting married had to bury her grandmother two weeks ahead of her wedding.

Rich's great-aunt turned ninety in May and had a very nice housewarming on the weekend of the funeral. This great-aunt has now been diagnosed with a fast-spreading cancer, and I know that Rich has probably seen her for the last time. He visited with her during his leave in August of 2008. She was so happy to see him and is very proud of him for the role he plays in Iraq.

During May, I noticed that we were losing another large spruce tree to the north side of the house, and I worked on getting another one brought in. This was no simple feat considering we wanted a fifteen to sixteen-foot tree replaced, and they would have only a certain window of time to bring it in and over the sod that was already laid! I had to take pictures of the dig site, send them to Rich, and then get on the line with him as the tree finally went in. Our regular landscaper worked with me after that to finish and patch up the front yard and landscape the site where the new tree was located. This was another long and tedious process.

This was all happening at the same time that our neighbors to the north decided to move back to Tennessee. They had had enough of the cold and dreary weather in South Dakota. This was also very disheartening, as they were young professionals and felt that this city didn't offer enough for a young couple like them.

I started a new Bible study group at home in spring with a couple of close friends, and this has been a very encourag-

  Linda J. Johnson

ing and uplifting activity for me. These girls have become close prayer partners and confidantes. God always seems to know when there is a need for me, and he fills it according to his perfect will. These gals understand, and they lend a sympathetic ear to anything that seems to be bothering me. We meet every other week, and it keeps me focused on just who is in control!

Meanwhile, back in Iraq, Rich was bringing two newer guys to chapel with him, and he said it was rewarding. He asked me to get some more books and devotionals sent to him for the men, so I got busy with that project! Rich was also getting concerned due to the fact that the site he had worked at now for almost three years would be making major changes.

The company was bringing in a second unit of men to take over various other technical repairs for the army's equipment. This group would be the DS shop, whereas Rich's group was the org/maintenance.

From the moment the new guys got there, Rich reported that the politics began. This was so disheartening to him because for the previous three years the men at D-2, for the most part, had gotten along and worked harmoniously together. There wasn't much back-biting or other negative activities going on among them, and they actually formed as close of a bond as possible under the circumstances. This was all about to change.

Rich's best friend, Terry, was fit to be tied. He couldn't believe that the company would stand for new men to come in and override those who had been there long term. Rich reported that a new female was put on-site located nearby them at D-2. She was supposedly oversight for LSI personnel and employed by the company that holds the contract. The problem with that plan was that she treated the men as if they were secondhand employees from the start. She took possession of some of their vehicles and began to institute rules over them. This went over like a lead balloon.

From that point on, Rich's phone calls became more distressful. He wasn't adjusting well to all of this, and Terry had decided to take the Blackwater position. Rich knew that Terry would probably take the new position because of what was happening within the company. I began to pray for Rich for endurance and for his adjustment.

He had been filling in for Terry again as the QAQC while Terry was in the U.S. for a leave. He only had a few altercations with the new men on-site, and just kept on doing his job, but he was stressed. I couldn't wait for his next leave. I knew he was going to be tired. He would need lots of rest and relaxation.

I also knew my husband well enough to know that if his best friend was going to leave the company, he would be discouraged. So, we began to pray for God's perfect will for Rich. Terry promised Rich that if he took a position at Blackwater, he would recommend Rich for a position also. I knew from that point on that I had to support Rich in whatever decision he made for his future. This would affect our lives. Rich assured me that the new position he would accept, if it were offered, would be inside the Blackwater compound and not be mobile throughout Iraq or outside their own compound. His understanding was that he would be a mechanic for the vehicles only and not required to go on any missions or carry any weapons. I am sure that Rich considered this position

     Linda J. Johnson

due to the close relationship he had built with Terry. This type of relationship bond, built in extreme conditions, is one no one else would ever understand except for someone who has been there. I would trust Rich's decision.

CHAPTER 43

During this time, I also made a decision to return to the original church that Rich and I had attended after we were first married. We hadn't stepped foot into Faith Temple Church for the past eighteen years, and yet, I was still seeking to find fellowship spiritually, that I hadn't yet found in Sioux Falls.

It was a good move. The pastor and his wife, Pastor Jeff and Rhonda Hayes, came out for lunch, and we discussed the ministry they had built upon there. This has become our church home for now, and we can see the growth of the people in many ways. It would be harder for me to just be a part of a congregation that Rich and I weren't leading. We are still working our way through this transition. Due to the nature of this ministry, however, I can feel at home there, and this was the original church where we were both called into full-time ministry.

The church has been very supportive of Rich and his mission in Iraq. They have posted his picture and address on the board and have been faithful to pray for him throughout this process. They also included me in prayer with an almost uncanny understanding of my need for support and encouragement.

Rich's family had the annual Fourth of July picnic at the lake, and a great-nephew was home visiting from Japan. He was stationed there with the air force, and I enjoyed speaking with him about what his uncle was doing in Iraq. He hasn't seen a tour himself, but he volunteered! I told him that I knew he would go if asked. Unfortunately, a lot of the conversation got touchy within the family because of the politics of 2008.

There is now a wide chasm and split within Rich's family that has occurred due to the past presidential election year. For the first time in my adult life, I have watched as division has happened due to party political lines being drawn within his family. Nothing upsets me more than this. I'm shocked at how uncomfortable it can get now if anyone brings up the topic of the past election. We cannot find a common ground or much to agree upon; the split is complete and the differences are stark!

I oftentimes think that when someone is criticizing this war, they are actually criticizing legitimate careers and jobs of men and women who volunteer to do what they are doing. Those deployed aren't complaining, and they aren't criticizing the careers and jobs of those who are home in America. Yet, to me it's the same thing. Why is one any less honorable than the other? I guess if we want to, we could find fault with every person's livelihood, including those public servants who

  Linda J. Johnson

live off of our tax dollars in local and state government, or at federal government, along with a bloated Congress! This would be a lot of Americans who are gainfully employed, with the taxpayers footing the bill. Yet, we don't hear the same criticism of them. I just don't get it.

I had a discussion with a local city-council member over the course of the summer. He attempted to tell me what he thought of President Bush and said that he was in support of our troops and all, but not the effort. It was the same old rhetoric, to which I told him that I didn't appreciate the increased taxes and out of touch city council and county in which we live, and could we focus our discussion there. Again, I get so tired of having to hear all of this, yet our voices are never heard. We remain the silent majority, or worse, we are persecuted and ridiculed, because we have our own opinions on the matter. I really related to a quip from the scrapbook of the most recent weekly standard magazine. The scrapbook went on to mention a line spoken by one of the characters in one of the Charles McCarry's great spy novels, "They have made Mr. Nixon stand for evil and they think that all it takes to be virtuous is to hate him. It is the sin of pride."

As a welcome respite from a chaotic year, I heard from friends and former colleagues of ours from Honolulu. They wanted to come for a visit to South Dakota right before Rich would get in. I was thrilled for the visit and the diversion!

The Bocobos got here on July 7, and we had a whirlwind visit. We toured Sioux Falls to start. They loved what they saw of this little city in the middle of the prairie! Then we headed out for the Black Hills and the Badlands. We stayed at my sister's home. They loved Mount Rushmore, and we shot pictures of a live buffalo nearby to our car inside Custer State Park!

It was so interesting to see South Dakota through their eyes. When someone hasn't been to this part of the country, we locals get to see what they see that maybe we have missed! The weather cooperated, and it couldn't have been more perfect.

My sister Cathy, as usual, was the perfect hostess at Rapid City, and we enjoyed our short stay there. I don't think I have ever seen Mount Rushmore in more beautiful weather. My thoughts weren't far away from Rich, however. He called almost every day on the cell phone to check in on us and see where we were and what we were doing. I knew he was missing the visit with them. I kept reminding him that he would be home soon and be able to get away from all the chaos inside Iraq!

We spent three days at the Black Hills and then came back through Mitchell, South Dakota, to have lunch with my mom and visit the Corn Palace there. All of these experiences were unique to the Bocobos, and they were taking it all in. We got some wonderful pictures and accomplished lots of personal projects while they were here!

Their last weekend in South Dakota was filled with going to church, where they were cordially greeted and introduced. Then we made the rounds and visited with Rich's relatives. It was a fun-filled and packed eight days. The fifteenth of July came around too fast, and it was a sad day to have to see them off again. We parted knowing that only God could decide when we would see each other again.

Meanwhile, Rich was bothered because sure enough, Terry had left the company to transfer over to Blackwater.

  Linda J. Johnson

At the same time, James, the administrator, put in his notice to leave during the time Rich would be home on leave. It appeared that Rich would be the last long-term guy from their Houston class still deployed at D-2!

One positive decision that was made in the middle of his darkness was that he received assignment to Terry's old room and would no longer be required to have a roommate. The new program manager in Iraq had visited D-2 and made the announcement that Rich had earned the right to have his own bunk as long as he remained deployed. Rich made a fifth move of his personal belongings right before this leave. This was tiring for him again and a hassle! He told me that he didn't even have enough time to unpack before he had to pack to leave for home.

CHAPTER 44

Another trial that Rich was going through was that he had been told by the QAQC Iraq coordinator that he should apply for the QAQC job at D-2 that Terry had vacated. Of course, he decided to do this, but no paperwork came through, and a week before he was due to come home, the job was posted. He didn't know what to make of this. He had done this job for almost three years inside Iraq and received awards pertaining to his work, and now he was supposed to apply or interview again for the same job he was doing! The pay wasn't even much of an increase, and frankly he was insulted. I told him to just calm down and go through the process, and hopefully they would get to him before he got home. It wasn't to be.

In fact, as Rich prepared to get transferred and go through all of the steps to get out of Iraq to come home on leave, he ran into another snag! At the BTC, he was all prepared on his second day there to get called up for his scheduled flight to Dubai from Baghdad airport when a notice was posted on the board. I mentioned earlier that all flights were cancelled due to Barack Obama's plane being there at the airport, and the airport was closed. What a shock and disappointment. Rich called and told me, and I flipped out! How could this happen?

We scrambled while the company rearranged his flight schedules, and he wouldn't be getting into Minneapolis until later on Friday afternoon. I reminded him that we had a second ticket and that he needed to get into Sioux Falls; however, the company wouldn't help him with that at the BTC. So, I had to phone Delta and tell them what had transpired. Graciously, they helped me due to Rich's whereabouts and rescheduled his flights for Friday evening without a change fee or charge.

Rich calculated that possibly up to one thousand people were bumped from Baghdad airport, and their leaves were disrupted due to this incident. I was sure that the press wouldn't report this. I was right, and they didn't. Not too many people knew that a lot of good people's lives were disrupted while the senator from Illinois visited the war zone. We had plans and had anticipated the return of our loved ones for months, and now we were all put on hold and reliant upon the mercy of the airlines.

Rich didn't get in until late on Friday evening. He was exhausted but happy to be home. His leave had only been extended by twenty-four hours, so he lost half a day or more at home from his original leave plans.

In addition, on the day that Rich was supposed to finally arrive home, I received a strange phone call from Iraq. The

  Linda J. Johnson

new administrator at D-2 called and told me that Rich was scheduled for an interview for the QAQC position for the following morning at 3:20 a.m. I told him that Rich would probably not be making that phone call, because he was still in the air and hadn't even reached the States yet. It appears that on base they didn't even have Rich's new scheduled flights, and hadn't heard a word about what was going on with the disruptions. I told them about it, and scanned his tickets and sent it all in. Then I called into HR direct at the BTC, to inquire about this interview. They told me that they would take care of changing the schedule and that Rich could interview at a more convenient time, like early morning here instead of in the middle of the night.

He interviewed on early Sunday morning, for the same job he had been performing and filling in for during the previous three years! He was still so jet lagged that he didn't know or actually even stress out over what he was saying. He considered it all so ridiculous.

Once again our leave was disturbed, and he wasn't able to get Iraq off of his mind when he got home due to this interview. He had been delayed long enough at the BTC that it would've appeared that the company could've sat him down right there to get the interview before he left Iraq for this much-deserved leave!

Rich received a phone call from the QAQC Iraq coordinator, and the phone call was a message congratulating Rich on his promotion! He still hadn't heard a word from anyone at his site by the time he left back to Iraq, and he hadn't received the paperwork required for his new promotion. We both just gave it up knowing he could straighten this out when he got back in. This time he needed his downtime at home. He had had enough stress in the past four months and didn't need any more to follow him home.

Interestingly enough, Blackwater approached my husband while he was home with an offer for a possible opening as well. He responded by sending in the required paperwork and waited to hear what would happen. So, when he left, we were both wondering what would happen with his future in Iraq. I knew that it was his desire to work with his buddy Terry, and my prayer was that God would keep Rich in the center of his perfect will. He is okay with staying or transferring over with them. So, that is okay with me.

When Rich finally heard back from Blackwater, they had put a hiring freeze on the position that they wanted him for, so he will wait for another opening with them. Terry is still trying and hoping to get Rich moved over there, especially in lieu of the changes going on inside Iraq.

Chris and the kids got here the evening following Rich's arrival. He had gotten some rest and was very happy to see all of them. The grandkids enjoyed eating out on the deck and grilling. We all went to church, and this was a good reunion for both Rich and Chris. It was a short but nice visit with them. Chris was encouraging his dad to do whatever was the best for him and to not listen to anyone else regarding what he wanted to do in Iraq. I agreed.

The first week Rich was in and after the kids left, we got doctors' appointments out of the way, and Rich puttered around the house. We got to walk together and make some tentative plans for a future leave, and he finally relaxed in his home. There wasn't much else to do now with the house at

  Linda J. Johnson

the two-year mark, and he could enjoy working in the yard and outside in the garage. I speculated on what it would be like for him to really come home for good!

We made a conscious decision on that leave not to include so many visits and gatherings. Our good friend and former elder, Floyd Thomas, from Kansas City, did come up and spend two days with us. He hadn't seen Rich since the summer of 2005, before Rich's original deployment. We really enjoyed showing him around the city and taking him to church. This helped Rich to relax and have fun even more than usual, and it almost felt like he was really home for good.

The weather was perfect for that leave. We got beautiful, sunny days and calm evenings. He and I both enjoyed just staying around the house and getting into a normal routine. It got much harder to think about his return to Iraq.

The morning of August 9 got here way too fast! We took our time and enjoyed a leisurely brunch before heading out to the airport. We had enough time there to enjoy refreshments and just reminisce about his time home. We prayed and asked the Lord to guide us for the upcoming days. I felt somewhat restless because I didn't know what Rich would go back into or what course he would follow in the days ahead.

We both were dreading his going back. He would only have an eighty-minute layover in Amsterdam, and this was bothering him. At Minneapolis, he called me, and we stayed on the phone almost the entire four hours of his layover there ahead of the flight to Amsterdam. I wanted to make sure that we got everything discussed because soon we would be back to quick phone messages and I would have to pick and choose and try to remember exactly what to discuss with him when he phoned. I dreaded the thought of this again.

My body finally gave up and gave in when he was on his flight from Minneapolis to Amsterdam. I slept deeply and fitfully. I didn't know when I would hear from him and when he would arrive inside Iraq or at the BTC. It would be much longer than I thought. I didn't receive a phone call from him until Tuesday morning. He was delayed leaving Dubai because he said the company was backed up. So, he did get rest going back, and he would need it.

CHAPTER 45

Rich is in the QAQC job now permanently, and the new site manager gave him his promotion on base after Rich got back to Iraq. He was surprised to find out, however, that they had moved him out of his office and put him in a much smaller space without ever consulting him while he was home. So many changes had gone on while he was home on leave. As he told me about them in his last phone call, I could hear the stress, once again, in his voice.

Also, when he got onto his base and job site, he found that one of the changes included the banning of cell phones for everyone, a rule made by the company that holds the LOGCAP contract, which is currently being questioned by the military contractors. The army continues to be able to use their cell phones on the same bases. When he finally called for a longer phone conversation, he told me that one of the first adjustments we would have to make was that he couldn't have his cell phone turned on at work. They were giving them walkie talkies to use instead and just for the job! This would now be how they would communicate with each other.

I was crushed in my spirit knowing that this would cause a difficulty for us because psychologically I could always reach him on his own line for three years at any time day or night. We would now have to count on speaking to each other before or after work shifts.

I already knew that this would prove difficult whenever I just wanted to hear his voice. He reported that the morale of the men had fallen sharply since he left. Once again I couldn't understand why the company or anyone else would want to heap more problems on these guys. They were already far away from home and loved ones, and some of them, like my husband, had put in years laboring for the company. There didn't seem to be rhyme or reason behind rules changing and hardships placed upon the families. We are now in a very serious place regarding his deployment and praying for the future. God knows what Rich should do and what lies ahead for us. I will have to dig deeper in my faith to find the peace I will need.

Rich told me that he is concerned lately because inside Baghdad, the company that holds the contract has laid off 200 men or downsized that many positions. Because his company is the subcontractor, people employed in similar jobs there must now compete with the contract holder employees and go through an interview process to retain employment inside Iraq.

I asked him if this affected the mechanics yet, and he said it didn't. My stress level has now accelerated because I am con-

  Linda J. Johnson

cerned that they are possibly going to let men go or force people out and place third-country nationals into open jobs. We have always believed that as the politics heats up, the jobs and positions will be affected. It looks like this activity has started in earnest. The men are all walking on pins and needles now.

We are also concerned with him staying on for the future because our portion of the costs is increasing significantly. I told him that we will continue to just take one day at a time. He said, "We will go from one leave to the next." He's right.

CHAPTER 46

A very nice project came my way right after Rich got back inside Iraq. I was delegated as the Minnehaha county coordinator for the "Cry Out America" event, which was held at the Minnehaha county courthouse on September 11. This proved to be a very worthwhile activity. The guidelines to organize this event came from the national Awakening America Alliance group, and I threw myself into the project. Again, Faith Temple Church picked up the project with me, and only a small committee of five joined me in putting this event together in a very short time.

Our one-hour program conducted from noon to 1:00 p.m. included local pastors, laypersons, veterans, a color guard, and politicians. Everyone focused on our founding fathers and the inheritance they gave to America, and then we reflected on the tragic events of September 11, 2001, that had united our nation. We included prayer inside the program meant to motivate Americans to turn back to a time of unity such as 9/11, and a call for prayer inside our country now.

We had about two hundred people in attendance, and we are in preparation and planning already for next year to repeat the event. Another very important highlight of our program was the singing of our national anthem and some patriotic songs, by a local high school, featuring a cappella small group. Everyone joined them during this time.

This national Christian non-partisan event went on in every state and every county across the U.S.A. Some had smaller groups of people attending at their respective court-houses with no organized program.

We were featured in a *Faith News Network* article after the event was over. The local TV stations and media played clips from our September 11 gathering throughout the evening news on September 11, 2008, as well.

At about this same time, my doctor scheduled me for an oral mouth surgery at the hospital to remove two rapidly growing bones that would eventually obstruct any future dental work. The first surgery was completed in August and didn't heal correctly, so while I was working for over six weeks on the September 11 project, I was in excruciating pain from the surgery. The second surgery was completed after the program, and this time it healed!

I called upon the Davidsons again to assist me during both surgeries, as well as our niece, Laurie. They were at the hospital with me, and my mom came over after both surgeries to stay and help me out at home for the first couple of days. Again, I am so thankful to all of them for being there when

  Linda J. Johnson

I needed them, and Rich says he can never repay everyone who has been there for me at times when he couldn't be.

The Davidsons actually insisted that I go down to their lake home on Lake Okoboji in Melford, IA, to recuperate for four days after my mom left, after surgery number two, in order that I would really rest and they wanted to take care of me. This getaway helped ensure that healing for me, and it worked! I had a wonderful, relaxing time as they pampered me throughout my stay. We discussed Rich's upcoming leave and the fact that he would be home for Thanksgiving and our thirty-first wedding anniversary. Although they would be gone to their winter home in Arizona, I knew we would be in communication with them throughout Rich's upcoming visit.

As I complete this book up to this point in our journey, I am happy to report that Rich has told me he will come home for good in 2009! He is putting his résumé out for recruiters, and he is exploring all job possibilities, including any that may come his way where we can stay in Sioux Falls. My hope is that he will be able to stay right here inside the home he has provided for us and find employment locally despite the downturn and shortage of jobs nationwide right now.

Right before this last leave, Rich told me that a new company will take over at D-2. We were shocked. The company is going through a RIF (reduction in force) right now inside Iraq, and hundreds of employees will be coming home by the end of the year. They have no choices and few options. No one knows who will be laid off and who will be retained. The company has offered JPAP (job placement assistance program), but for many, that would mean they must move themselves to where the openings are. In fact, Rich brought home two documents that were supposed to explain to current employees what is happening written in a question and answer format. Both documents are seven pages in length in small print, and a person would possibly have to have a law degree to figure out what the company is saying. We are all unsure as to ramifications of the transition within Iraq for LSI at the end of December 2008.

In Iraq, Rich's company will be giving up nine sites and retain only five by the end of December. So, we have begun to pray for guidance for our decision because, although Rich's contract is good through August 2009, he could be one of the men who is not kept with the transition. I reminded him that I believed this had happened due to the past election and all companies were looking to go "leaner," but we both feel that his level position and all the mechanics are needed as long as our military is in there.

I am very happy to report that our little church has completed a wonderful Christmas project for Rich and the forty-nine other men at his site. These guys were so surprised when they received the Christmas Craftsman toolboxes filled with goodies and other needed items. A lot of businesses and other groups helped with contributions for these boxes, and we raised every bit of the funds needed to get the boxes shipped in.

I know that this year these gifts have had a special meaning for all of them, as they all contemplate their own future. Many of them will never be together working on the same site again and at holiday time. They deserved something extra special. At least they were made aware that they are prayed for and remembered fondly by some grateful Americans for the jobs they perform and the service they render to our troops!

Rich got to get up in front of the church and congregation at both services the first Sunday of December and thank the congregation for the support. He was also able to reconnect with the grandparents of the last South Dakotan killed in Iraq this past year. They were so happy to speak with Rich, and they reminded us that we had been Sunday school teachers for that young man when he was in the second grade! Rich told them that Jeremy's death was not in vain.

We spent our thirty-first wedding anniversary at the post office helping get that shipment of boxes out to Iraq. Then, on December 5, we said good-bye once again. I sent him back to Iraq after a restful fifteen days at home.

Somehow, I have a peace that everything will turn out all right for us too. Rich has done an exemplary job, and he has held up his head inside Iraq. Whenever he decides to come home, I believe he will have something waiting for him here, and we will be able to get on with our lives. In addition, our story will be told.

I'm tired right now, but I'm proud. We are weary, but we will stay this course. We are on target to reach our personal financial goals to see a day when Rich can come home. I am very proud of my husband and my son. They have sacrificed for this country. They have sacrificed for our family. They have been obedient to their own personal call and answered that calling in a way that they could.

I would like to close this story with an example of a typical day in the life of my husband inside Iraq:

5:30 a.m. (wake up) He has to take his turn brushing his teeth and using the restroom, which is shared with three other men.

5:45 a.m. He walks over to the mess hall, or dining facility, for breakfast. Breakfast for Rich is usually cereal, juice, or an egg plate. He reports that they do not have real eggs most of the time, so that is something he misses from back home.

6:20 a.m. Finish breakfast and walk back to their work site on base.

6:30–6:45 a.m. Sometimes he calls me at this time, which is around 10:30 p.m. my time, just to check in or say hi. He will call earlier now due to the cell phone restrictions.

6:45–7:30 a.m. They have morning report anytime during this time slot. Sometimes the meetings are short, and sometimes they take longer. The agenda is set by the foreman, and "toolbox" topics are discussed for that day. They also receive some instructions for the current day or previous day's work. When an important upper management visitor is on-site, they have a variation of the daily meeting. Special packages or group distribution of boxes sent especially for the unit is done at this time.

7:30–11:30 a.m. Work scheduled on vehicles. Mechanics go to their bays, and Rich is available to help any of them out. He rotates between the guys' bays and his office to take in incoming vehicles or send them back to the army. Rich also takes over for the foreman when the foreman is on leave. He is able to stand in for all of the positions, other than the administrator's job, on-site.

11:30 a.m.–12:30 p.m. Walk over and back from

dining facility for lunch. Sometimes the guys make personal phone calls here, if necessary, at the phone facility. Also, Rich will take his laundry once per week to the laundry people during his lunch hour. He will drop it off and pick up in a day or two. He gets a receipt for what he has given them to ensure pickup. They all know each other quite well now, and the laundry workers know our men. The laundry workers work for the parent company in Iraq and are sometimes Americans but mostly are TCNs (third-country nationals).

1:00–5:00 p.m. This is regular work duty on the vehicles. They finish jobs begun, or new jobs come in dependent upon the army's coming and going.

5:00–5:30 pm. Afternoon report is held. This is a follow-up meeting held to discuss the day's activities, and any alerts or other topics are discussed. These report meetings are also a type of roll call to account for everyone's presence. During all meetings, anyone can bring up subjects they want to discuss or clarify.

5:30–7:00 p.m. Finish up, clean up, and end the day on the work site. Finalize all day's paperwork for vehicles worked on and finished. Correct paperwork is very important on the charging of hours for payment.

7:00–8:00 p.m. Walk over and back to the dining facility for dinner. Again, the choices are varied and food is plenty. However, Rich reports that it all tastes the same due to the oils used there. He can tell when cooks are changed. The change reflects itself in the taste of the food. Rich is a fussy eater and likes food plain. He says lately they have been using lots of onions and spices on everything! Therefore, he sometimes stays in his quarters and eats one of his microwaveable dinners that have an American taste. This also allows him to have time away from the same men that he spends so much time with already. He tries to unwind.

8:00–9:30 p.m. Rich showers and then watches TV on the nights he doesn't phone me. (Rich now has cable TV with some American channels on this base.) If he has a scheduled phone call to me, he has to shorten his own personal time for himself. The phone center is a short walk, and he is already tired from a long day and will have a short night.

9:30–10:00 p.m. Lights out…He sleeps through the night unless there is an incoming alert or a room inspection. When the alerts come at night, they must dress and rush out to a hardcover building until the all-clear. During a room inspection, he is awakened and must go outside until inspection is complete; however, these are infrequent. A loudspeaker and sirens would go off to alert them to take cover if necessary. Sometimes I phone and wake him up when he is just falling asleep, if I have something I have to ask him. I try not to do this often, due to the fact that I know he needs his rest.

Rich reports that their downtime is so short, and they work so many hours. Therefore, he doesn't take advantage of the gym facilities on the base. Once in a while on payday, they take the vehicle right after work and drive over to the larger PX area off base, but down the road, and still in the Green Zone. They have dinner at Burger King or one of the fast food restaurants at the PX. This is a big night out for them!

  Linda J. Johnson

They must do all their shopping at the PX for any personal items that we don't send to them.

Sunday nights after work, Rich rushes to his quarters to shower and change. Then he goes to chapel. The chapel service helps him focus on his faith. He especially enjoys the current chaplain that is assigned to his base. I ask him why he doesn't go to the weeknight Bible studies held at the chapel, and again he reports that he is too tired to do anything but work, eat, and sleep.

Of course, the monotony of many of the days can be changed when there is an incident nearby, like a bombing and/or explosions. They also change schedule when someone is visiting and when extraordinary problems occur with the vehicles. They may have to take a longer time to fix or deliver a finished product than they anticipated. Also, if they get an alert during the day, this changes their schedule. Lately their days are interrupted by constant sandstorms.

Once a month, if they aren't too busy, they schedule a Sunday afternoon cookout. This is a time of preparing and eating a meal together within their housing area, and it is designed for fellowship among the men. They oftentimes receive their awards earned during these venues. All of the men contribute to the cost of the food purchased, and someone cooks it or goes and picks it up. They decide together what they want. This helps them bond without the pressure of their work assignments.

I like it when he tells me that nothing is going on. To me this is a relief. It gives me less worry and stress when he is calmed down and it is business as usual inside Iraq. He will discuss any issues or problems with me during our longer phone calls, and we pray about them together. We reverse roles frequently during these calls. Sometimes he is calming me down, and sometimes I am calming him down! This long-distance marriage has to be worked on like any other arrangement. He is strong for me when I need him to be, and I am strong for him most of the time.

We recently discussed the Georgia/Russia conflict, and I told him that I was worried about all of those men from the country of Georgia, many of whom he worked with and had become a part of their lives. We don't think we will ever know what has happened or will happen to them in this national crisis for their families. We can only pray for a peaceful resolution.

EPILOGUE

As this book is going to press, Rich has been moved to BTC/Liberty/Victory base at Baghdad's airport. He has been retained by the company during this time of RIF. This was a lateral transfer for his QAQC position. When he got the offer to take this job and stay with the company, he had two hours to give them his response. He called me. I told him, "You have to do what your gut tells you. You have always made good decisions inside Iraq, and I believe you will now do the same. God is with you there."

He didn't like leaving D-2. It had been his home for over three years, and now he finds himself waiting for permanent housing, and he is sleeping in a tent! It is cold, according to him, and he has to start all over again with new relationships. I know I won't settle down back here until I think he has settled in over there.

He has told me that he will stay in Iraq as long as he has to. He will stay as long as there isn't a job for him back home. When I mention that I want to go in too, he tells me he needs me here. He wants me to hold down the home front so he can do what he does. He said recently, "You are the reason I keep going on."

For that reason I will go on. I will pray daily for the continuing strength, endurance, and wisdom that my husband needs to do his honorable job. I pray for a bright future for us post-Iraq. I pray he'll find a good job so he can live out his old age in the home he has provided for us.

I pray every day for the families of all of our men and women serving in Iraq or Afghanistan, in whatever capacity they find themselves in. I also pray for the Iraqi people who want peace and democracy for their country, and for those who have stood at the side of our men.

I continue writing to be a voice speaking out of the shadows for our families. Although we are just one family who has chosen this lifestyle, I believe many other families will relate to what I have written here.

People will wonder in the days to come why anyone would continue through the hardships of contracting in the first place. At this point in America's juncture, these Americans are compelled to go. Many of our loved ones feel this is the best way for them to feed their families, contribute to America's mission, and further their own careers with companies that could keep them employed during an economic downturn. Contracting gets "in your blood," and a network of relationships opens up for them due to the experiences these contractors have, along with a special bond between

  Linda J. Johnson

them that no one else has with them. We might say that they are closer than brothers. They have experienced hardship and endured trials together, which caused them to form that unique bond known only to them, unlike any other job environment. Certainly Americans who get up and go to their jobs inside our country cannot completely relate to this unless we attempt to tell them what it was like.

The quality and diversity of people they have worked with, who come from all walks of life, is fascinating, and they all now represent a part of America's history. When stories are told for the future generations about Iraq, our stories cannot be left out. Our loved ones' contributions to the effort must not be forgotten. So many of them are home now, but they are still silent and faceless.

It has been stated that there are over 190,000 contractors inside Iraq in 2008, and if so, then they outnumber our military by 30,000. I want these men and women to stand up for the right they have had to go and do their jobs, whatever they may have done, and be proud of their service. Their families deserve the respect of other Americans who haven't experienced this conflict.[1]

An additional reason I am writing this book is for Rich. He will have a more cohesive and complete picture of what this journey has been like for me. He already says that he thinks I have it worse than he does (especially regarding the wait and the monotony or problems to solve). He doesn't envy me managing this home and its unique problems. He is really good about remembering to appreciate me and reminding me that he understands it is hard on me too.

Many of our loved ones who are deployed to Iraq or

Afghanistan will move on to other countries eventually and be those ex-pats working outside of America especially in this day and age of high taxes. They believe that this type of work will give their families maximum earnings for their hard work. For the sake of their children, they sacrifice the comfort of home. None of them will ever be anything other than American through and through. Call them patriots!

We feel more than a kindred spirit with all of the families of those who have sent a loved one into OEF or OIF on behalf of this global war on terror.

As for me, it is very simple. "...In sickness and in health, for better or for worse...till death do us part."

Linda J. Johnson

ENDNOTES

Chapter 15

1. Griffe White, "Contractors Rarely Held Responsible for Misdeed Done in Iraq," Washington Post, Nov 4, 2006, p.A12

Chapter 22

1. Patrick Cockburn, "Revealed: Secret plan to keep Iraq under US control, Bush wants 50 military bases, control of Iraqi airspace and legal immunity for all American soldiers and contractors," Independent World, June 5, 2008.

Chapter 24

1. Monica LaBelle, "Man searches for gift in Iraq, finds friends," Argus Leader, September 18, 2006, front page.

Chapter 31

1. Sid Jacobson and Ernie Colon, The 9/11 Report, a Graphic Adaptation (New York: Hill and Wang, a Division of Farrar, Straus and Giiroux, 2006), 112
2. Col Austin Bay, comment on "Army Releases Captured War on Terror Documents: Al Qaeda Offers Medical and Vacation Benefits for Terrorists: Austin Bay Blog, comments posted February 17, 2006. http://austinbay.net/blog/?p=929
3. John McCain, "We Must Win Iraq War and Not Just Withdraw," Journal Constitution, July 24, 2008, news.

Chapter 32

1. LSI, Jack List e-mail message to author. June 20, 2007.

Chapter 33

1. Jennifer Parker, "Contractors Profit," Army Times, June 4, 2007, Opinions/letters.
2. Linda Johnson, "Contractors Give, too," Army Times, July 2, 2007, Opinions/letters.

Chapter 34

1. Sgt. Amber S. Fitz, "Civilians in Iraq for money," Argus Leader, July 14, 2007, Voices section/letters.

2. Military Statistics, "Iraqi War Casualties," 2003–2006: Iraqi War Casualties (per capita) (most recent) by State, http://icasualties.org/oif/

3. Veterans for America, "Our National Guard, Too High a Price," 2007–2008   http://www.veteransforamerica.org/wp-content/uploads/2008/07/our-national-guard-too-high-a-price.pdf

4. Jon Tevlin, "Contractors fight a war within the war," Minneapolis StarTribune, August 12, 2007.

Chapter 35

1. LSI, Jack List e-mail message to author September 9, 2007.

Chapter 36

1. Ted Roelofs, "Blackwater Founder Eric Prince defends defense contractors," The Grand Rapids Press, May 20, 2008.

2. Erik Prince, "We can take those lumps." Army Times, July 21, 2008, Vol. 69 Issues 1, 18–19 2p

3. Philip Ewing, "Blackwater May Protect Shipping Firms," Air Force Times, Nov 10,2008, Vol 69 Issue 17 pg 33

4. Editors, "Big Boy Rules' shows extent of mercenaries' role," review of Big *Boy Rule,* by Steve Fairanu, Army Times Book Review, Nov 24, 2008, pg 32.

5. Donna Leinwand, "Islamic charity leaders guilty of aiding Hamas," USA Today, Nov 25, 2008.

6. The Hebrew University, Jerusalem, Israel, "THE CHARTER OF ALLAH: THE PLATFORM OF THE ISLAMIC RESISTANCE MOVEMENT (HAMAS), 1997, translated by Raphael Israeli, http://www.fas.org/irp/world/para/docs/970824.htm

Chapter 39

1. Ali Gharib, "US/IRAQ: A Blueprint for Withdrawal," IPS News, June 25, 2008.

Epilogue

1. Editors, "Big Boy Rules' shows extent of mercenaries' role," review of *Big Boy Rule*, by Steve Fairanu, Army Times Book Review, Nov. 24, 2008, pg. 32.

BIBLIOGRAPHY

Bay, Austin Blog The. http://austinbay.net/blog/?p=929

Cockburn, Patrick. "Revealed: Secret plan to keep Iraq under US control, Bush wants 50 military bases, control of Iraqi airspace and legal immunity for all American soldiers and contractors, Independent World, June 5, 2008.

Colon, Ernie and Sid Jacobson. *The 9/11 report, a graphic adaptation*. New York: Hill and Wang, 2006.

Editors. "Big Boy Rules' shows extent of mercenaries' role," review of *Big Boy Rules*, by Steve Fairanu, Army Times Book Review, Nov. 24, 2008, pg 32.

Ewing, Philip. "Blackwater May Protect Shipping Firms," Air Force Times, Nov. 10, 2008, Vol 69 Issue 17 pg 33

Fitz, Amber S. Sgt. "Civilians in Iraq for money." Argus Leader, July 14, 2007, Voices section/letters.

Gharib, Ali. "US/IRAQ: A Blueprint for Withdrawal," IPS News, June 25, 2008.

The Hebrew University, Jerusalem, Israel. "THE CHARTER OF ALLAH: THE PLATFORM OF THE ISLAMIC RESISTANCE MOVEMENT (HAMAS), 1997, translated by Raphael Israeli, http://www.fas.org/irp/world/para/docs/970824.htm

Johnson, Linda. "Contractors give, too." Army Times, July 2, 2007. Opinions/letters

LaBelle, Monica. "Man searches for gift in Iraq, finds friends," Argus Leader, September 18, 2006, front page.

Leinwand, Donna. "Islamic charity leaders guilty of aiding Hamas," USA Today, Nov 25, 2008.

McCain, John. "We must win Iraq war and not just withdraw," Journal Constitution, July 24, 2008, news.

Military Statistics. "Iraqi War Casualties," 2003–2006: "Iraqi War Casualties (per capita) (most recent) by state." Iraqi War Casualties http://icasualties.org (accessed June 8, 2006)

Parker, Jennifer. "Contractors Profit," Army Times, June 4, 2007. Opinions/letters.

Prince, Erik. "We can take those lumps." Army Times, July 21, 2008, Vol. 69 Issues 1, 18–19 2p

Roelofs, Ted. "Blackwater founder Erik Prince defends defense contractors," The Grand Rapids Press, May 20, 2008.

Tevlin, Jon. "Contractors fight a war within the war," Minneapolis StarTribune, August 12, 2007.

Veterans for America. "Our National Guard, Too High a Price." http://veteransforamerica.org (accessed July 5, 2008)

White, Griffe. "Contractors Rarely Held Responsible for Misdeed Done in Iraq," Washington Post, Nov 4, 2006, p.A12

ABOUT THE AUTHOR

Linda J. Johnson received her doctorate in Christian education in 1999. She also holds certification as a CISD counselor. She is an ordained minister and an internationally-endorsed community services chaplain with Church of God, Cleveland, Tennessee.

Currently Linda resides in Sioux Falls, South Dakota, where she contributes to the community as a substitute teacher and a contracted mentor who helps disabled adults with test-taking, while awaiting the return from Iraq of her husband of thirty-one years.